Anita Diamant's
The Red Tent

CONTINUUM CONTEMPORARIES

Also available in this series:

handwritten: £1.49

· ANITA DIAMANT'S

The Red Tent

A READER'S GUIDE

ANN FINDING

continuum
NEW YORK · LONDON

2004

The Continuum International Publishing Group Inc
15 E 26 Street, New York, NY 10010

The Continuum International Publishing Group Ltd
The Tower Building, 11 York Road, London SE1 7NX

www.continuumbooks.com

Printed in the United States of America

Library of Congress Cataloging-in-Publication Data

Finding, Ann.
    Anita Diamant's The red tent : a reader's guide / Ann Finding.
        p.   cm.—(Continuum contemporaries)
    Includes bibliographical references.
    ISBN 0-8264-1574-1 (pbk. : alk. paper)
    1. Diamant, Anita. Red tent.   2. Dinah (Biblical character)—In
literature.   I. Title: Red tent.   II. Title.   III. Series.
PS3554.I227R43   2004
813'.54—dc22   2004011876

Contents

The Novelist

Anita Diamant was born on June 27, 1951. She grew up in Newark, New Jersey, in a Jewish neighborhood, with a younger brother. Her mother, Helene, and her father, Maurice, who was a linotype operator, were both Holocaust survivors who met in a refugee camp in Switzerland. The family moved to Denver when she was 12. It is surprising, given her considerable involvement with Judaism later in her life, that she did not have a religious upbringing and received no formal Jewish education. Her family did not observe Jewish ritual beyond "lighting Hanukkah candles and holding an annual family Seder" (anitadiamant.com).* She attended the University of Colorado for two years, and then transferred to Washington University in St. Louis, where she gained a B.A. degree in comparative literature. She also has an M.A. in American Studies from the State University of New York in Binghamton. She has lived in the Boston area since finishing her university studies.

Diamant's first ambition was to be an actress, although she later wanted to be a university teacher of literature. She started to write

---

* The "Seder" takes place during the first two nights of the holiday of Passover and is an important family gathering.

poetry while she was a graduate student, and cites several poets among her literary influences: Pablo Neruda, Walt Whitman, and William Carlos Williams. Aware that few poets make an adequate living, she turned to journalism as a career in her twenties. She had a poem published in *In These Times*, a Democratic Socialist paper based in Chicago, then took a post at *Equal Times*, an alternative women's weekly publication produced in Boston, before later working at the *Boston Phoenix*, which describes itself as "New England's largest arts and entertainment weekly." In her role as assistant to the editor, she was relegated mainly to secretarial work, but she has described her time there as when she learned her craft: "Sometimes, it is worth it to take jobs that are just jobs—you never know where they will lead" (Friedland). She gradually moved on to write features and a regular column. In 1980 the *Phoenix* sent her to report on a nudist camp. She produced an article described by the *Boston Globe* as "[v]ery funny, and meant to be" (August 30,1980), displaying a youthful sense of humor that is not always apparent in her later work. She consolidated her career as a journalist with the *New England Monthly*, where she was a contributing editor, the *Boston Magazine*, and the *Boston Globe*, for which she wrote a column in the Sunday magazine from September 1988 until November 1994. In addition, she has written for many publications, including *Parenting Magazine*, *Jewishfamily.com*, *Reform Judaism*, and *Hadassah Magazine*. Since 1985 her journalistic writing has been primarily about contemporary Jewish practice.

The many articles that Diamant wrote in two decades as a journalist often provided valuable material for her fiction and her books on Jewish life. Her regular column for the *Boston Globe* Sunday magazine was, she says, a "gift" (Friedland). In her final article, on November 20, 1994, she said: "I've written about everything, more or less: dogs, taxes, abortion, racism, trust, friendship, bargain-hunting, child care, AIDS, garlic, and raspberries." This list of topics sums up neatly the diversity of interests that are also revealed in Diamant's fiction: concern with the big moral, political, and social issues of the day, side by side with an intimate attention to the delicate intricacies of human interaction. As she says in this article, in her work she

> was forced to pay attention to big seismic shifts (the fall of the Soviet Union, the twenty-fifth anniversary of the birth-control pill, the gun-death epidemic) and subtle transformations (the opening of a new library, the day my daughter walked to school alone for the first time, the weight of words spoken to friends in mourning).

Although Diamant has said that "it's not a goal of mine to be a writer about women" (washingtonpost.com:live online), and she has repeatedly denied having any feminist agenda, her passionate interest in women's lives and their achievements is evident in her journalism. A lengthy piece published in the *Boston Globe* on August 5, 1984, entitled, "The Spirit and Stamina of Fordie Madeira," celebrated the fortitude of a woman nearing forty that combined marathon running with the care of triplets, and having had to cope with the death of her husband from cancer after only five years of marriage. Finding happiness, peace, and self-fulfilment against the odds is one of Diamant's major preoccupations.

Before the publication of *The Red Tent*, Diamant was known for her journalism and her series of nonfiction books on Jewish life, which she sees as her "Life Cycle" books because together they cover most aspects of life from birth through marriage and parenthood to death. The first three books, *The New Jewish Wedding* (1985), *The New Jewish Baby Book* (1988), and *Living a Jewish Life: Jewish Traditions, Customs and Values for Today's Families* (1993), of which the last written with Howard Cooper, were published before she started work on her fiction. *Choosing a Jewish Life: A Hand-*

book for People Converting to Judaism and for their Family and Friends (1997) appeared in the same year as *The Red Tent*. It is at once a reference book, giving prospective Jews information about preparations, rituals, and ceremonies, and a personal address to converts, written in an informal and accessible way. The preface tells Diamant's own story. It was only when she met Jim Ball, who in 1983 became her second husband, that she realized how strongly she felt about being Jewish and raising a child in accordance with Jewish traditions: "I knew myself to be utterly and unconditionally Jewish" (xviii), she stated, but her knowledge of Judaism was limited. Her interest in pursuing a Jewish education, in which she was supported and accompanied by Jim, ultimately led to his conversion and Diamant's acquisition of "an authentic Jewish identity" (xix). They were married as "really two new-minted Jews" (xx). Jim's conversion, and her own reflections on her identity as a Jewish woman, were the inspiration, or at least the starting point, for Diamant's series of books that continued with *Saying Kaddish: How to Comfort the Dying, Bury the Dead and Mourn as a Jew* in 1998 and *How to be a Jewish Parent* (2000), which she wrote with Karen Kushner. Diamant had her only child, daughter Emilia, in 1985.

The Red Tent

Diamant started thinking about *The Red Tent* when she turned forty. After nearly two decades of journalism, she wanted to explore a different kind of writing. She found writing fiction a great challenge: "It's more open-ended. I have confidence in my nonfiction . . . I know what that kind of book is shaped like. With novels, you don't know where they're going to go. All writing is a process of learning" (Kanner).

In search of ideas for fiction Diamant turned, as other novelists have before and since, to the Bible. She was initially interested in

Rachel and Leah, Jacob's wives, but later became fascinated by Leah's daughter, Dinah, whose story is told in Genesis 34 (see Further Reading for the full biblical text). The attraction of this tale for a novelist is easy to understand because "it has sex, violence, plot, drama, suspense, and an unexpected bloody dénouement" (Justice).

For a woman writer, however, there are further intriguing elements in this and many episodes of the Bible in which women play a part. It was Dinah's silence that gave Diamant an opening. Women's experiences and their perspective on events are almost entirely absent from the Old Testament; choosing to make Dinah the narrator of her story allowed for the imaginative creation of Dinah's point of view. In a discussion with former priest and fellow writer James Carroll for *Book* magazine, Diamant spoke of her desire to give voice to biblical women and also to foreground experiences central to women's lives that are not recognized in the Bible:

Sex is part of life—I mean, if you write about life and you leave sex out, then you've left out a major part of it. There's a lot of food in *The Red Tent*. There's more food than sex, as a matter of fact. To not write about food, to not write about sex, is not to talk about women's experience (Diamant and Carroll).

A talk given to the Jewish Women's Collective emphasized her intention to give life to the everyday existence of her female characters. She cited Virginia Woolf's assertion that literature has had nothing to say about the lives of ordinary women before the tenth century: "'*The Red Tent* answers Woolf's challenge,' Diamant said. 'I wanted to write about the lives of women in the ancient world—not Jews, but women'" (Gilman).

The silencing of women, or the failure to acknowledge their existence, is a theme taken up by other women writers who have found inspiration in biblical stories. In her novel, *Only Human* (2000),

British writer Jenny Diski focuses on Sarah (or, originally, Sarai), wife of Abraham, from Genesis 11–23. In childhood Sarai is loved, but, as a girl, given no status in the family. When her father makes a ritual recitation of the names of the forefathers, he identifies her brothers, but excludes her, the youngest child: "[T]here was always a pang at the final name that was never spoken. No mention of Sarai" (Diski 23).

The only reason that Dinah is mentioned in Genesis at all is because she is raped, thereby unwittingly bringing about the terrible vengeance inflicted by her brothers on the tribe of her attacker. Diamant found enough ambiguity in the telling of the rape to replay the incident as a love affair and to turn Dinah from victim into a woman with control over her own life. Although perhaps taking a risk in making substantial changes to a sacred text, Diamant was confident that the Jewish concept of *midrash*, a creative reading that attempts to explore what is mysterious and unexplained in the Bible, would allow, even encourage, bold readings: "'It's up to us to figure out what it means, it's incumbent upon us to make sense of it—it's not a hands-off experience, and that's where I come from, in terms of giving me permission to do whatever the hell I want'" (Clark).

Several other novels about biblical women have been published since *The Red Tent*. Angela Elwell Hunt's *The Shadow Women* (2002) revisits Moses and the women around him: his mother and sister, and his wife, Zipporah. India Edghill's *Queenmaker* (1999) turns to 1 Samuel in the Old Testament for the story of Michal, daughter of King Saul and wife of David.

Diamant's approach to writing fiction drew on her methods of working as a journalist, through research. Biblical research was not her priority, although she would have had many opportunities to engage in the discussions about the Bible that are part of Jewish practice. She instead undertook historical research in order to find out information about how women lived 3500 years ago. In addition to finding out about clothes and food, she investigated remedies for disease and women's medicine: midwifery, contraception, and abortion. Research was helped by a visiting scholarship in the Women's Studies department at Brandeis University and a library fellowship at Radcliffe's Schlesinger Library that gave her access to the Harvard Library system. She spent three years writing the novel, regarding it as a "hobby," with no assurances of publication. With a characteristic love of community, she joined a small women's writing group when she embarked on *The Red Tent*; it met regularly once a month, and she continues to be a participant.

The extraordinary success that *The Red Tent* achieved over the two or three years after its publication in 1997 brought Diamant recognition she could not have anticipated. She was in constant demand and admits to overworking during that period. In addition to making many appearances to talk about *The Red Tent*, she was writing her second novel, *Good Harbor*, which took her four years, and continuing to publish her nonfiction work. Diamant accepted her fame with pleasure, but was not unduly affected by it. Interviewers regard her as a calm and modest woman, "[u]npretentious, grounded, and thoughtful" (Friedland), who continues to live as she always has, unaltered by material gain: "[S]he says only that 'now my daughter can go to college wherever she likes'" (Clark).

Good Harbor

With *Good Harbor*, Diamant risked the displeasure of her many admiring readers by not writing another biblical interpretation. She made a deliberate choice to change direction in terms of content and context, even though the focus on women and the relationships between them remains paramount. She states on her website: "I don't seem to have another biblical novel in me. Not now and not for the foreseeable future." *Good Harbor* is a contemporary story of the developing friendship of two middle-aged women living in the Massachusetts beach town of Cape Ann, where Diamant actually rented a house while she was writing the book. One of the two central characters in the novel, Kathleen Levine, is diagnosed with breast cancer at the start of the six-month period the novel covers; the most convincing parts of the novel are those which deal with her treatment and her responses to it. Like *The Red Tent*, it is an affirmative story. Despite the problems faced by both of the protagonists — the other, Joyce Tabachnik, has a difficult adolescent daughter, a distant husband, and is struggling to write — a positive conclusion is reached. Kathleen is going to survive, and both women are on better terms with themselves and their families. Diamant again undertook research, but this time by talking to friends and visiting an oncology clinic. She described breast cancer in an interview as "part of the landscape for women" and as a disease that "raises all kinds of issues about femininity and identity and sexuality" (Jernigan), which are issues that she explores in the novel. To Ellen Kanner she said: "Breast cancer is one of the great fears of women of our time. We're all waiting for it to happen to us." Her concern was evident nearly a decade before in one of her columns for the *Boston Globe* (October 18, 1992), covering the second annual Massachusetts Breast Cancer Coalition march and rally that highlighted the devastation caused by the disease to women and those around them.

Simon and Schuster published *Good Harbor* in the United States in October 2001, very shortly after the horrific events of September 11 and the subsequent national and international turmoil. Regular book tours were suspended at this time, with all attention on terrorism rather than on new fiction. Diamant could have been expected to feel apprehensive about the fate of her new novel, but she told Suzanne Mantell that she had confidence, based on her experience with *The Red Tent*, in the "slow and steady build"; "'I have great readers.'" It did indeed sell steadily, but it did not achieve the success of its predecessor. *Publishers Weekly*'s annual hardcover ratings for 2001 placed it in the category of sales greater than 150,000, but it did not make the Top 30 list, which would have put it in the weekly charts. The novel came out as a Scribner paperback in 2002 and was recorded in *Publishers Weekly* as having sold in excess of 100,000 copies in that year. It was published in the United Kingdom by Macmillan in September 2002.

A few fans did not appreciate the new novel, but in an interview with Alex Clark in *The Guardian* Diamant asserted, "they're beginning to forgive me for switching." She anticipated that readers would find the same qualities in *Good Harbor* that they responded to in *The Red Tent*: "What I hope readers take from the book is the importance and crucial nature of women's friendships, which are undervalued and underappreciated" (Mantell).

Good Harbor was reviewed a little more attentively than *The Red Tent* in the United States, but without conspicuous enthusiasm. The excitement that had been generated by *The Red Tent* provoked expectations that were not fulfilled. Merle Rubin, in the *Christian Science Monitor*, thought it "not a very good novel" and "something of a disappointment, not only in style but in imaginative substance." The *Washington Post* reviewer perhaps summed up the feelings of goodwill toward the writer of *The Red Tent* in suggesting that *Good Harbor* "is a novel that you desperately want to like—but can't." There were those who found merit in it. Robin Vidimos, in the *Denver Post*, praised its "keen emotional insight," comparing Diamant's work with Anne Tyler's. Judith Wynn, in the *Boston Herald*, described it as an "amiable contemporary novel," but found weakness in the "vague" male characters. The *Boston Globe* reviewer, Karen Campbell, generally liked the book, discovering perhaps an echo of the evocative rendition of women's relationships present in *The Red*

Tent: "It stands as a crystalline illumination of the inner worlds women share only with one another."

Reviews in Great Britain were more consistently appreciative. Sally Morris thought it a "life-affirming read" (*Sunday Mirror*), and Geoffrey Wansell in the *Daily Mail* found it "immensely moving and delicately told," crediting Diamant with the "rare ability to tell a gentle story with charm and sensitivity." Declaring himself a "middle-aged man" and thus not one of Diamant's usual fans, he was nevertheless "entranced by every word of it."

There are moments of cliché and melodrama in *Good Harbor*, "the stuff that Hallmark cards are made of" (*Washington Post*), and the novel does not have the intensity and conviction that mark out *The Red Tent*, but Diamant's compelling storytelling skills—especially in the sections relating to Kathleen's cancer treatment—are nevertheless undiminished, as is her ability to animate the everyday friendships of ordinary people.

Since *Good Harbor* Diamant has been working on a third novel that is different again from the previous two. With the (provisional) title, *Dogtown*, it is set in early nineteenth-century rural Massachusetts, necessitating research into "nineteenth-century dentistry" and "looking at drawings of ladies' underwear and shoes of the period" (anitadiamant.com). Another nonfiction book, *Pitching My Tent: On Marriage, Motherhood, Friendship and Other Leaps of Faith*, was published in October 2003.

The Novel

STORIES AND STORYTELLING

Biblical Sources—The Red Tent *as* Midrash

Historically, the rabbis used this highly imaginative form of storytelling to make sense of the elliptical nature of the Bible—to explain, for example, why Cain killed Abel. The compressed stories and images in the Bible are rather like photographs. They don't tell us everything we want or need to know. Midrash is the story about what happened before and after the photographic flash (Diamant, Picador study guide).

The Red Tent has stories from the later parts of Genesis as its source. Part One of the novel, "My Mothers' Stories," opens with Rachel rushing from the well excited by the wild stranger she has met who, she says, kissed her and intends to marry her. The parallel for this in the Bible is in Genesis 29:10–12, where a much briefer account is given of Jacob's arrival at his uncle Laban's settlement, after having been sent out by his father, Isaac, to find a wife from within the family. With considerable addition to detail, this section of the novel continues to follow Genesis quite closely through Jacob's marriages, first to Leah, then to Rachel, and his many years of work for Laban to pay for his brides. The births of ten of Jacob's sons, by Leah and the handmaids, Bilhah and Zilpah, take the story to 30:20. Diamant's first part finishes with the births of Dinah (30:21) and Rachel's long-awaited son, Joseph (30:22–24).

Part Two, "My Story," shows Jacob's cunning in building up his own stocks of sheep and goats, his dispute with Laban, the journey of Jacob's family to Canaan and Laban's pursuit, Rachel's theft of her father's holy images, and the meeting with Esau (Genesis 30:25–end of 33). Genesis 34 is the story of Dinah and Shechem (Shalem in the novel); 35 tells of Rachel's death giving birth to Jacob's twelfth and last son, Benjamin, and of the forbidden relationship between Reuben and Bilhah. In this section Diamant makes many additions to the story; for example, the visit to Rebecca that has no place in the Bible. Part Three, "Egypt," is essentially Diamant's invention. In the Bible Dinah is never again mentioned after 34:26 when Simeon and Levi "took Dinah out of Shechem's house and went out." No hint is ever given of what might have happened to her next; her experiences in Egypt are Diamant's imaginative reflection on the consequences of Dinah's brief love affair. Dinah's meeting with her brother, now Zaphenat Paneh-ah, in Chapter 4, alludes to the story of Joseph, told in the Bible from 37 on and off until the end of Genesis, but gives a rather different interpretation of his adventures.

The Jewish practice of *midrash* arises from the condensed, suggestive, and often poetic nature of the Bible. The stories make an appeal to the reader's imagination and curiosity because so much is left unsaid. They are, in narrative terms, full of "gaps" that enable readers to interact with the text to produce their own readings for discussion. Interpretation of the Bible is also made more difficult, or perhaps more interesting, by the problems of translation. Crucial words often are subject to intense debate to establish their meaning. The Bible can therefore be a rich source of ideas for fiction, and

Diamant has chosen a provocative incident to place at the heart of her novel. In a sense, however, only part of *The Red Tent* is *midrash*. As Dinah's story takes on its own life and direction, the links with Genesis become looser, and Dinah gradually transcends her source to become a rounded fictional character in her own right.

The kind of reading that *midrash* represents, which gives readers licence to make their own interpretations, is a special version of the processes that are common to all reading. There are always openings for a range of interpretations that depend heavily on a wealth of factors (for example, personal, cultural, or political), even in a more transparent text than the Bible. Diamant is similarly not the only writer to become fascinated by a minor character in a dramatic story and to wish to foreground what is hidden in the shadowy background. The impulse to write a character's story from a different point of view from the one dominant in the original text has appealed to others, particularly (although not exclusively) women writers.

A notable example of a rewriting of a well-known fiction is Jean Rhys' novel, *Wide Sargasso Sea* (1966), which takes Rochester's wife, Bertha Mason, from Charlotte Bronte's *Jane Eyre* (1847), and traces a sequence of events which could lead to her ending her life locked in the attic of Thornfield, defined as a madwoman. Rhys' perspective changes the dynamics of the original novel, emphasizing Rochester's power and the innocence of Antoinette (whom Rochester names Bertha, against her will). Rochester's status as romantic hero is severely dented by Rhys' representation of him. Daphne du Maurier's *Rebecca* (1938), which is itself to an extent a reading of *Jane Eyre*, has been revisited by both Susan Hill and Sally Beaumont. Hill's *Mrs. de Winter* (1993), is, like Part Three of *The Red Tent*, a consideration of what happened next, a sequel to *Rebecca*. Many readers must have wondered about the life the second Mrs. de Winter spends with Maxim after they are virtually exiled from England at the end of the story. Even more subject to readers' spec-

ulation is the eponymous Rebecca, already dead at the start of the
novel, but a powerful presence in the story nevertheless. Rebecca's
account of events is lost but Beaumont's *Rebecca's Tale* (2001), as
the title suggests, is an attempt at redress.

Interpreting a sacred text as Diamant does in *The Red Tent* is a
bolder enterprise perhaps than radically revising a novel, even
though such novels as *Jane Eyre* have become almost sacred objects
themselves for some readers. In part a filling out of events in Genesis, *The Red Tent* also poses a challenge to the text in its repositioning
of perspective, which gives priority to neglected female experiences.
In her interpretation of Genesis, Diamant has made both obvious
changes and additions to the biblical story and more subtle shifts of
emphasis.

The most significant change that Diamant has made to Genesis
is in the number and character of the women. Women in the Bible
are mentioned only if they need to be. It seems unlikely, for in-
stance, that Dinah is the only surviving daughter born to Jacob, but
she is the only one to whom anything happens, justifying a minor
role in the tale. Diamant gives names and identity to the mothers of
Rachel, Leah, Zilpah, and Bilhah, who are not referred to in the
Bible, and makes all four of Dinah's "mothers" biological sisters, not
just sisters-in-law. Laban is said to have two daughters in Genesis,
Leah and Rachel, even though some interpreters before Diamant
have argued that Zilpah and Bilhah, described in the Bible as "con-
cubines" or "handmaids," may have been his children, too. Although Rebecca appears earlier in Genesis as Isaac's wife and is
remembered for her part in Jacob's tricking his father into giving
him the blessing that should have gone to the elder twin, Esau, she
has no role in the sections on which Diamant works. Her death is
not reported; it is the death of Isaac that is told in 35:27–29. Her
appearance in *The Red Tent*, as an awe-inspiring matriarch and oracle, might be imagined from the forthright way she speaks to her

sons and husband in the Bible, but her original role was a secondary one. There are many female characters that have no parallel at all in Genesis: Ruti, the last woman Laban takes as wife; the midwife, Inna; Werenro, Rebecca's slave; Tabea, Dinah's cousin who becomes her friend; and Meryt, the midwife who helps Dinah give birth and remains a constant companion and surrogate mother. All of these female characters, even those who play a limited part, have great importance in relation to Diamant's purpose in the novel.

Other alterations are in the detail and affect the interpretation of biblical events. One significant revision concerns the way Diamant treats the rivalry between Leah and Rachel. The substitution of Leah for Rachel as Jacob's first wife is Laban's doing in Genesis. Jacob serves him for seven years to earn the right to marry Rachel, but, when the time comes, Laban "took Leah his daughter, and brought her to him" (29:23). Laban carries out this deception because Leah is the elder daughter: "It must not be done in our country, to give the younger before the firstborn" (29:26). Diamant's placing of responsibility with Rachel and Leah themselves, who conspire because of Rachel's fear of her wedding night, highlights the lack of power of the biblical women who have no choice in their destiny. Diamant gives Rachel and Leah some control over their lives, although the success of their plan is still dependent on Jacob's complicity. Jacob's preference for Rachel over Leah is obvious in Genesis. Leah's fertility is explained as a gift from God; the bearing of many sons may cause Jacob to love her better. In 33:2, when he sees Esau approaching with four hundred men and is fearful for the safety of his family, Jacob places those he loves best, Rachel and Joseph, at the back: "And he put the handmaids and their children foremost, and Leah and her children after, and Rachel and Joseph hindermost." Leah is described in 29:31 as "hated" though some translations soften it to "unloved," which reduces the implied hostility. In *The Red Tent* Rachel remains the best-loved wife, but Jacob is seen to treat Leah, and his lesser wives, with respect and consideration. Leah has an accepted and important place as first and elder wife. When Jacob introduces his sons to Esau in Part Two, Chapter Four, he begins with those born to Leah (p.155).

Central to *The Red Tent*, if not to Genesis, is the "rape" of Dinah by Shechem. The King James version of Genesis 34 tells that when "Shechem the son of Hamor the Hivite, prince of the country, saw [Dinah], he took her, and lay with her, and defiled her" (34:2). Being defiled would mean becoming both unmarriageable and unfit to worship God. Other versions use the more specific word "rape." Despite the apparent simple brutality of this statement, the story is sufficiently ambiguous, even contradictory, to merit a different interpretation of Shechem's behavior. Shechem says that he loves Dinah immediately after the assertion of rape and wants to marry her, as would be necessary to uphold her honor. Speculation also arises too from the opening verse of 34: "And Dinah . . . went out to see the daughters of the land," suggesting an adventurous, perhaps even a reckless, spirit. The verses are cryptic, but Diamant translates these few short sentences into a fully reciprocal love relationship that is understood and condoned as a preliminary to marriage by Shalem's family, although not her own. Reuben, the most conciliatory of the brothers in the novel, points out to Jacob and his sons (p. 235) that Dinah did not cry out and has not been abandoned, both of which would be required for an accusation of rape; however, Levi and Simon are determined to see Dinah as the victim of "desecration."

Dinah is given significance in *The Red Tent* that far exceeds her marginal role in the Bible. The reverse happens to Joseph, whose story occupies a lengthy section of Genesis and is written in a much more coherent narrative form than the earlier parts. The biblical narrative of Joseph begins in Genesis 37 and, apart from a brief interlude about Judah and his wives in 38, and an account of Jacob's death, continues until the end of Genesis (Chap. 50). Genesis concludes with the death of Joseph, stressing his importance. Joseph's story is a familiar one that has found a place in popular culture. As Jacob's youngest and favorite son, he is treated preferentially and arouses the resentment of his brothers. He has prophetic dreams about his future dominance over his brothers who attempt to kill him, but instead sell him into slavery. Finding himself eventually in Egypt, he becomes the slave of Potiphar, one of the pharaoh's officers. A series of events brings him to the court of the pharaoh, where Joseph's ability to read dreams raises him to a position of power. He does meet his brothers again and is reunited with them, but not before they have bowed down before him as he predicted, in ignorance of his true identity. Having punished his brothers for their treatment of him, he forgives them and promises to take care of them.

This vivid tale is told in part by Diamant, but as an anecdote that minimizes Joseph's importance as Israel's savior by showing him as an arrogant and weak man. The brother who was once Dinah's "constant companion" and "truest friend" (p. 89) is perceived as a "barbarian" by Re-mose, who despises his illiteracy. Shery, the woman who attends Dinah when she falls ill after helping with the birth of Joseph's son, speaks of him with gossipy disrespect, claiming that he is "truly an arrogant son of a bitch" (p. 341). She is also scornful of the pompous name he has adopted, which means, "'The God Speaks and He Lives,'" The effect of her chatter is to undermine the exalted status Joseph is accorded in Genesis; this is reinforced by a humorous alteration that is made to the biblical story. In Genesis Joseph is imprisoned for sleeping with Potiphar's wife. It is a false accusation from a woman who has tried and failed to seduce him. In *The Red Tent*, however, Shery presents an embroidered story worthy of contemporary tabloid newspapers in which Potiphar finds the lovers in bed together (p. 342). Dinah has difficulty maintaining interest in Shery's story and resorts to yawning and closing her eyes

in the hope of bringing the monologue to an end. Joseph is re-
deemed to some extent on meeting Dinah, but later in the novel,
when he demands that Dinah accompany him on a visit to their
dying father, she sees only a "self-absorbed man" (p. 362), who acknowledges that he is a "weakling" in need of his sister to hold his
hand.

Diamant has been accused of representing men unfairly in *The
Red Tent*, but it is rather that she translates them from epic heroes
into human beings, building on hints given in the elliptical stories
in Genesis to create credible characters. Some of the male characters in the novel are certainly contemptible: Laban, Simon, and Levi
are appalling in their greed and brutality; however, not all of the
male characters are the same. Shalem and his father, Hamor, are
represented as honorable men, and Benia, invented for the novel, is
almost a modern "new man" in his treatment of Dinah.

Diamant primarily emphasizes that men can be weak. Rather
than reinforcing a perception of the strong biblical patriarch, she
points up the fallibility and vulnerability of the male characters.
Jacob is on the whole represented sympathetically in *The Red Tent*,
as a decent and hardworking man doing his best for his family. His
dependence on the work of women, particularly Leah, however, is
repeatedly shown. One episode, a reworking of Genesis 32:22, may
serve to show how Diamant revises male characters. In Part Two,
Chapter Three, Jacob's tribe crosses the second of the rivers they
meet on the journey through Canaan. Jacob, left last to cross, spends
a night on the other side of the river from his family. He is discovered the following morning "beaten and naked"; what happened is
not explained. Jacob is considerably affected by his ordeal, whimpering in pain and calling for his mother. Inna and Rachel tend to him
"as though he were a swaddling baby" (p.146). Once he recovers he
has changed and become fearful, turning to Levi, the least reliable
of sons, for support. His response shows him to be human, trauma-

tized by a frightening attack. In the Bible, on the other hand, this is a crucial passage about Jacob's heroic struggle with God in which he proves himself: "as a prince hast thou power with God and with men, and hast prevailed" (32:28). It is at this moment that God gives Jacob the name, Israel. Far from being a sign of approval from God, the name Israel is seen by Dinah as a mark of cowardice, Jacob's way of disguising himself:

Jacob cowered and took a new name, Isra'el, so that the people would not remember him as the butcher of Shechem. He fled from the name Jacob, which became another word for "liar," so that "You serve the god of Jacob" was one of the worst insults one man could hurl at another in that land for many generations (p. 247).

The removal of God from the scene at the riverbank is indicative of the whole of *The Red Tent*. The world Dinah inhabits is not a monotheistic one. Although Jacob worships El, the God of his father and grandfather, his belief is not always apparent in *The Red Tent*. When he is attacked, he screams about blue river demons rather than feeling a heavenly presence. The guidance that God gives him in Genesis is absent from the novel; "fiery voices" in dreams call him back to Canaan (p.104), not a direct commandment from God. The women in the family seem almost to disregard the beliefs of Jacob, firmly committed to their ancient pagan gods or, especially, goddesses.

Stories and Storytellers

The Red Tent might be described as a *bildungsroman*, a narrative that follows the development from childhood into adulthood of one character, in this case Dinah. The *bildungsroman* (from German *bildung*, meaning education, or formation and roman, novel) is a common form for the novel, the focus of attention being on what the character learns, what she discovers about herself. Such novels often follow a rebellious character or one who makes many mistakes from which that character has to recover. Jane Eyre, in Charlotte Bronte's novel, is an angry, neglected child who, through harrowing experiences and the discovery of a man whom she can love, achieves a peaceful and happy life. In Dickens' *Great Expectations* the consequences of poor choices are spelled out in the story of Pip, who achieves maturity through hard lessons. Dinah does not share the unhappy childhood of Pip and Jane, but similarly embarks on a journey, both literal and emotional, that tests and changes her.

In many examples of the *bildungsroman* the story starts with the protagonist as a young child and ends in early adulthood. The difference in *The Red Tent*, however, is that Diamant extends the scope of the *bildungsroman* to include more of Dinah's life and the lives of those important to her; this is a feature of the family saga, which generally deals with several generations over many years. Beginning with Laban's offspring, Diamant's story shows the growing up of Jacob's family and beyond into the marriages and children of Dinah and her brothers, from before Dinah is born until after her death. It covers a long period of time, but how long is difficult to determine because the narrative is not precise about the passing of years. Jacob remains with Laban for more than twenty years, and Rachel waits fifteen years for the birth of Joseph during that period. Dinah is about thirty when she marries Benia, and she lives to be probably close to fifty. In all, the novel covers sixty years or more.

It is narrated in the first person, from Dinah's point of view, which makes the story both intimate and down to earth. The epic grandeur of the biblical original is not imitated in Diamant's narrative, although there are echoes of the language of Genesis. Language is straightforward to reflect a life that is lived in harmony with and dependence on the earth. Diamant avoids abstractions and complex sentences to create a narrative that is direct and readily accessible to readers. She uses such rhetorical devices as repetition to reinforce, devices that are also used in the Bible, especially in the parts of Genesis that run in parallel with *The Red Tent*:

And Jacob lifted up his eyes, and looked, and behold, Esau came, and with him four hundred men. And he divided the children unto Leah, and unto Rachel, and unto the two handmaids.

And he put the handmaids and their children foremost and Leah and her children after, and Rachel and Joseph hindermost.

And he passed over before them and bowed himself down to the ground seven times, until he came near to his brother.

And Esau ran to meet him, and embraced him, and fell on his neck, and kissed him: and they wept (Genesis 33:1–4).

The simple construction of these sentences, with repetition of openings and emphasis on verbs of action—"and he divided . . . and he put . . . and he passed over"—is followed in much of *The Red Tent*. For example, on page 48, consecutive paragraphs begin "Leah tried to stand . . . Leah pushed . . . Leah roared and delivered her son."

The novel is full of description that evokes sensory experience—sights, smells, and sounds. It is a tactile novel that attempts to portray the actuality of life. The description on page 48 of the birth of Reuben does not hold back on the detail, from the "strange red bubble" and "flood of bloody water" when Leah's waters break to the falling out of the placenta. The pain of childbirth and the animal quality of the experience are faithfully rendered, with Leah "panting and fearful" and "whimpering like a dog." The physical realities of existence in a tented camp, living in close proximity to animals, are foregrounded when Dinah returns from her stay with Rebecca at the beginning of Part Two, Chapter Six. The smell, the noise, and the brutish behavior of her father and brothers strike her anew in contrast to the feminine civility of Rebecca and her Deborahs: "They grunted rather than spoke, scratched themselves and picked their noses, and even relieved themselves in plain sight of the women. And the stink!" (p.199).

The words Diamant chooses carefully combine the contemporary with the archaic, making contact with modern readers while emphasizing the ancient context of the story. Characters are therefore said to be "pregnant," but are also described as "with child." Characters may be "making love" or "having sex," but Dinah also uses the biblical word "know," which is a euphemism for sex: "The day after Jacob knew Bilhah for the first time" (p. 63) relates to the time when Bilhah offers herself to Rachel as a surrogate mother so that Rachel can fulfil her dream of giving Jacob a child. When the offer is expressed to Jacob, she again uses an archaic word in suggesting that he "sire a child upon Bilhah, in her name."

The directness and plainness with which the story is told establish Dinah as a reliable narrator. The story gains power and credibility in the simplicity of its telling and the readers are encouraged to have confidence in Dinah's account. First-person narrators are by their very nature subjective, their story bounded by the limitations of their personal knowledge. Dinah's narrative, however, includes the thoughts and wisdom of many—particularly her mothers. Although she is a strong character, she seems to be a vehicle for the story as much as a director of it; the story belongs to her but is a celebration of, even a eulogy to, her mothers and by extension all women.

As with all stories told in retrospect by those who experienced the events described, there are moments when the adult narrator reveals a little of what happens later or what is to be the significance of an event. Just as narratives contain flashback (analepsis), in which an event earlier than those currently being described is related, or recalled, so can they also have anticipation (or prolepsis) that reminds the reader that the narrator knows the complete story already. An early example occurs on page 9, where Rachel is described as "small-boned and, *even when she was with child*, small-breasted" (italics added). Here her future as a mother is assured, although it is many chapters on that Rachel finally gives birth. At other times Dinah reminds readers that she is telling a story already known to her, as on page 44 where she says: "But I am rushing my story. For it took years . . ." In this story, of course, it is not necessary for Diamant to hold back information for the purposes of suspense. Many readers will know that Rachel was the mother of Joseph and Benjamin. The most unusual thing in this novel, however, is that the story includes and goes beyond Dinah's death. Readers will logically assume of a first-person narrative that the narrator cannot die; if she were to die, she would not be able to recount the story. Diamant, however, breaks this implicit rule by giving the aftermath of Dinah's death in the final few pages of the novel, still in Dinah's voice. This ending acts as a coda, a summary of later events, which brings the novel to a satisfying conclusion. Readers are able to find out what Dinah, once dead, could not have known—how she lived on in the minds of others and what happened to the people close to her. The story is in fact projected forward "unto the hundredth generation" through Re-mose's children and his children's children.

In an oral culture such as this—writing is only mentioned when Dinah reaches Egypt—information is communicated through story; family history recorded in the memory and passed down through the generations. There are all kinds of stories within the novel, and most of the characters tell them, either in private to one another or at family gatherings. Many of the stories are memories of events and people; others are tales of gods and goddesses that are kept alive through transmission. Stories are often told in the form of song or as accounts of dreams. They are sometimes perceived as prophetic, and sometimes express fears and preoccupations. Important occasions always involve both song and story, and the person with the highest status will always have a tale to tell. On the visit to Mamre, when

Rebecca speaks after the required feast, it is to tell part of her own life story (p. 181).

Second-hand, incomplete, or poorly understood stories exist alongside characters' tales of their own lives or of events they have witnessed, showing how stories may be changed in the telling. Shery's account of Joseph is mediated by her attitude toward him. With more positive intent, Meryt inflates Dinah's accomplishments in order to make her the legendary figure that Joseph is not permitted to be in the novel. When Meryt and Dinah go to live with Meryt's son, Meryt is determined to ensure Dinah's place in their new community. She spreads stories about Dinah's skills in midwifery and presents her to Menna and his family as an oracle, a woman to be feared. Throughout her friendship with Dinah, she tells a "fabulous tale" (p.281) of Dinah's life: "Thanks to Meryt, I became a legend among the local women without once venturing out of Nakht-re's garden" (p. 282). At the end of the novel, Dinah hears her own story told by someone else when she meets Gera, Benjamin's daughter. Dinah is consoled to find that her experience in Shechem was "too terrible to be forgotten" (p. 379), even if it has gained further tragedy over the years in the mistaken belief that Dinah "died of grief."

Dreams occur in the Bible as prophecy or evidence of the will of God. In *The Red Tent* the understanding of dreams is more in keeping with twentieth-century opinion. After Shalem is murdered, Dinah is haunted by nightmares in which she relives the terror of waking next to Shalem covered in blood. Other dreams relate to hopes and wishes, such as when the four sisters dream of Dinah's birth (pp. 78–79), or happy memories; after Meryt's burial Dinah dreams of her and of her other mothers (p. 359). Dreams that predict or determine the future are given credence (for example, Jacob's powerful dreams that draw him back to Canaan), but prophecy, or more precisely the role of prophet, encounters skepticism, too. As Shery points out, anyone could have done what Joseph did:

Everyone was struck by his princely bearing and by his ability to interpret dreams and divine the future. He told one poor drunkard that he would not live out the week, and when he was found dead—not murdered, mind you, simply done in by years of strong drink—the prisoners proclaimed him an oracle (p. 343).

It is worth noting too that Zilpah, who sees herself as "a kind of priestess" (p. 15), generally gets it wrong: "As usual, my auntie misread the signs" (p.168). It is only Rebecca who is attributed with real powers.

Those who are especially good at storytelling are admired and sought. In the absence of other entertainment, a well-told story is valuable. When Dinah and Joseph are young, they find themselves leaders among the children for a while, even in charge of those older than themselves. Because they were the "best at making up stories," their brothers treated them as king and queen. Stories enliven dreary days; Dinah remembers Leah telling her the story of the feast she prepared on Jacob's arrival "during dull, hot afternoons" (p. 19). Jacob, too, is a storyteller; Dinah describes him as a "weaver of words" (p. 73) when he tells the "terrible story of his father, Isaac."

The telling of stories has many important social and psychological functions in the novel. Diamant combines the benefits of the old oral culture with those of modern practice, in which articulating personal history is accorded therapeutic value. In this ancient community, stories maintain continuity between the generations, ensuring that family history is not lost. Telling, sharing, and exchanging stories is on many occasions a ritualized activity that imparts a sense of harmony and union. When Jacob finally meets Esau, the event he has dreaded throughout the journey, and they have had a meal together, the brothers tell two kinds of story, first recounting the story of their grandfather Abram, giving "the family history in proper fashion," and then reminding each other of their shared childhood. Such recollections unite the brothers and bring satisfaction to the listeners (pp.162–163), reinforcing their common heritage. Songs have a similar role. The singing that takes place at the big family gatherings works to rekindle social cohesion and to impart a sense of grand occasion. On the journey to Shechem, Zilpah's simple children's song spreads through the group to become a celebration of freedom from Laban. It is unusual in that everyone joins in—the men and the women singing together—breaking down the normal strict boundaries between the sexes (pp.129–130). In the telling of stories, there are usually "men's" stories and "women's" stories in a culture where men and women inhabit different spheres. Dinah knows the stories told by and to the men mainly by hearing them from Joseph.

Some stories, similar to those told to children as fairy tales now, are there to reassure and teach. When Dinah becomes frustrated about her inability to learn to spin, Bilhah is on hand to tell her the story of Uttu (the Sumerian goddess of weaving and spinning). As she tells the story to Dinah, she helps her with the spinning, conveying both the importance of the task and the way to do it.

In love, storytelling becomes a powerful means of communication. When Dinah and Shalem become lovers, telling of their families is a vital part of their coming together: "Whenever we were not kissing or coupling or sleeping, Shalem and I traded stories" (p. 226). Benia, too, tells Dinah everything about his previous life when they marry, although, significantly, Dinah does not reciprocate: "Benia did not ask for my story in return" (p. 330). Although their life together is built on communication—"Benia and I shared stories in the evenings. I told him . . ." (p. 331)—Dinah withholds the full truth of her past.

Not telling one's story causes problems and obstacles in relationships between characters. The story of one's family and one's experiences needs to be told and retold, or so the novel would have it. On the journey to Egypt to start a new life with Nakht-re, Re-nefer tells Dinah many stories of her own childhood—"charming tales and stories from her infancy" (p. 257)—but the story stops short at her arrival in Shechem. Dinah's hopes that she will learn more about Shalem are unfulfilled. Re-nefer's absolute silence about her son, a silence that "throbbed with pain," contributes to the distance that grows between the two women, as well as to Dinah's own reticence about her first marriage. The tragic hold that Shalem's death has over her life is broken only when Dinah begins to articulate her experiences to others—when she says it out loud. It takes three tellings for Dinah to come to terms with it. She first tells Werenro, who she meets for the second time at a banquet given for Re-mose. Thought dead, Werenro has in fact survived the attack that was made on her when she was a slave to Rebecca, but is horribly injured, physically and emotionally. The extent of her suffering is perhaps what unlocks Dinah's story; here is someone who can understand the depth of her pain:

Without hesitation I told her everything. I leaned my head back, closed my eyes, and gave voice to my life. In all of my years, I had never before spoken so much or so long, and yet the words came effortlessly, as though this were something I had done many times before (p.305).

It is made clear that her story has been festering inside for many years, ready and waiting to be expressed. The telling of it has an immediate therapeutic effect on Dinah: "I said 'Shalem' and my breath was clean after years of being foul and bitter. I called my son 'Bar-Shalem' and an old tightness in my chest eased" (p. 305).

The second time she tells her story is to Meryt, her trusted friend, after she has met Joseph and Re-mose has finally learned the truth of his past. The release gained by being able to reveal what Re-nefer always insisted must be kept secret enables Dinah to open up to Meryt. Again Dinah has a physical response to unburdening: "I was overcome by the understanding that I had spent a whole day without the weight of the past crushing my heart" (p. 356). Finally, she tells her husband, Benia, and the tale takes its proper place in the past: "[T]his time my heart did not pound nor my eyes fill as I told it. It was only a story from the distant past" (p. 357).

Dinah's Story

[Y]ou are Dinah, my last-born. My daughter. My memory (p.82).

Leah's pronouncement about Dinah at her birth indicates the importance of her role as the only girl in her generation to carry forward the female heritage she learns from her mothers. In the Prologue, Dinah describes remembering as a "holy thing" (p. 4); her task as teller of her own life story and those of her mothers gains a sacred status parallel to the recording of male experience in the Bible. Many commentators have noted that history has often been male-dominated—his-story not her-story—and Diamant alludes to this acknowledgment when Dinah directly addresses the contemporary woman reader who, she claims, is all too aware of the silences in women's history:

And now you come to me—women with hands and feet as soft as a queen's, with more cooking pots than you need, so safe in childbed and so free with your tongues. You come hungry for the story that was lost. You crave words to fill the great silence that swallowed me, and my mothers, and my grandmothers before them (p. 4).

Women's writing, as such literary critics as Elaine Showalter have pointed out, has always suffered from a lack of continuity as well as dismissal of its significance. In her influential book, *A Literature of Their Own* (1977), Showalter shows the ways in which women's writings have been forgotten, leaving writers of a later generation no forbears from whom to draw inspiration, no knowledge of the experience of those who have gone before. The links in the chain of tradition that binds one generation to the next are constantly broken; "each generation of women writers has found itself, in a sense, without a history, forced to rediscover the past anew, forging again and again the consciousness of our sex" (p.12).

The opening sentences of *The Red Tent*—"We have been lost to each other for so long. My name means nothing to you. My memory is dust"—are a strong declaration of both the history of silence on the subject of women's lives and the need to establish connections between women in the explicit reaching out from fictional character to reader. The choice of the word *we* as the first of the novel announces the re-creation of links that have been broken. Dinah's passionate prologue becomes almost a prayer that she concludes with blessings and "Selah," a word that often appears at the end of a psalm. Its original Hebrew meaning is uncertain, but it has been translated as "lift up voices" that would be appropriate here because Dinah is about to speak for all those women whose voices have not previously been heard.

Dinah's view of her place in biblical history is as a "footnote," her story a "brief detour," and her reputation that of a "victim" (p.1). Dinah's biblical status is as a classic female stereotype, the fallen woman. Fallen women are those whose apparent sexual misdemeanors have placed them outside the boundary of acceptable female behavior. Many of the women who are named in the Bible are included in this category, starting with Eve, who was held responsible for the first Fall, man's ejection from Paradise. In Genesis, Tamar, wife of Judah's son, Ur, earns a story in Chapter 38 because she prostituted herself to her father-in-law, through trickery, but with legitimate motive, and had twin babies by him. Diamant makes oblique reference to Tamar in *The Red Tent*, but gives her a new role as the Canaanite woman who saved Werenro after she was attacked: "Her name was goodness itself, Tamar, the sustaining fruit" (p. 305). The idea that female sexuality can cause mayhem is evident in the story of Helen of Troy, the beautiful heroine of Greek myth, desired by all men. Paris, son of Priam, the king of Troy, steals Helen away from her Spartan husband, Menelaus, an action that precipitates the ten-year Trojan War in the Greeks' attempt to reclaim her. Dinah's story is directly comparable to Helen's, although on a smaller scale, in that her sexual relationship with Shechem/Shalem leads to the eradication of an entire community. In accounts of Helen there are differing assessments of her culpability in the affair with Paris, some considering her a victim, others that she fell in love with Paris as he did with her. That ambiguity is in Dinah's story, too, as has been shown earlier.

Diamant's achievement in *The Red Tent* is to save Dinah from the sorry fate of joining the ranks of literature's fallen women, marked only by their sexual experiences, whether as victim or culprit. Sexual relationships with men are important in Dinah's account, but her life is also validated by bonds with other women, experiences of motherhood and work, and by her responses to change and to intense suffering. It is through the development of multiple aspects of her life that her maturing sense of identity and self-worth is revealed.

Dinah's journey in the novel is on one level a physical one. From a fairly isolated but secure life with her family near Haran (in present day Iraq/Syria), she moves south through the land of Canaan, a journey of several hundred miles, living for two years in Succoth. She stays for three months with Rebecca in Mamre, not long before her visit to Shechem (in Israel), when she meets Shalem. From Canaan Dinah moves to Egypt with Re-nefer, an even longer journey by boat, leaving from Joppa, sailing across the Mediterranean Sea, and down the river Nile to her destination, Thebes. She remains there for many years before her final move with Meryt to the Valley of the Kings.

For most of her life subsequent to the migration from Haran, she exists as an outsider who observes cultural practices very different from those of Laban and Jacob's camp. Her dominant experience after the murder of Shalem is of having to create a place for herself in communities where she is a stranger. Even before that, at Mamre, Dinah feels uncomfortable with Rebecca and unimpressed with the Deborahs' "life with the Oracle" (p.193); she is relieved to return to her mother's tent. Her role in Thebes, although she is the mother of Re-mose, is at first that of nursemaid; her displacement is apparent in her adoption of the garden as her home. Once Re-mose has left his grandfather's house, her position is never quite assured because she and Re-nefer no longer have anything in common. She fully regains fully the sense of belonging that she had as a child only when she finds a home with Benia: "My house was a world of my own possession, a country in which I was ruler and citizen, where I chose and where I served" (p. 327).

In childhood, as the youngest of Leah's children, and, in her mothers' view, additionally blessed because she is a girl, Dinah has a privileged position in the women's world to which she belongs. Male children are denied the red tent after they are weaned, but Dinah continues to have access to her mothers and their tales long after she is of an age to leave. Thus, she gains confidence in the early part of her story that she will always be loved and protected, even when she has to face the inevitable realization that she is not the center of Leah's world and that she, too, will have to grow up to learn to live with a "divided heart," sharing her love (p.102). She has already learned ambivalence, as all children do, a little earlier when she is confused by her momentary hatred of a mother she completely loves (p. 93). Throughout this learning process, Dinah's belief is nonetheless unshakeable that she is cherished, indicated by her understanding of gods and goddesses. In Chapter Two, Dinah reveals her childlike view of the gods as an extended family, additional uncles and aunts who have no problems and are "interested in everything that happened to me" (p.108).

Her early years are relatively free from stressful events; one of the few challenges she faces comes with the discovery of the corpse of Ruti, whose death is the first she has witnessed. Her immature understanding of lives that are not as cosseted as her own precipitates a reaction of anger mixed with distress at the submission that, she feels, has been the cause of Ruti's misery and, ultimately, her suicide. Dinah feels contempt for Ruti's weakness in not standing up to Laban, failing to appreciate the powerlessness of Ruti's situation.

The atmosphere of security and safety provided by her mothers allows Dinah to embrace the journey away from her home to a distant and unknown place with eagerness. The journey to Canaan is described at some length in the novel. Dinah takes great pleasure in the novelty of traveling and quickly forgets her old life, "rooted in one place" (p.131). As first-person narrator, she focuses attention on the people and events that are of most interest to her. Her fascination with the great rivers they cross and the strange people they meet, her sense of life opening up for her, are illustrated by the precision of the detail, as in her description of the crossing of the river. The freedom she is given and the new perspective on her family accorded by the relaxation of the boundaries between the men and the women make the journey dreamlike, a "time out of life" (p.130). Dinah says, "I loved every minute of the journey to Canaan" (p.134). In contrast, an experience that she enjoys much less—the visit to Rebecca at Mamre—is given little space, with only "pale and scattered memories" to report back to her mothers (p.190).

On meeting members of her extended family at the end of the journey, Dinah encounters some of the complexities of life, and of difference, which have not troubled her previously. Tabea is the first female friend of her age and Dinah is thrilled by the prospect of confidences shared with someone like herself; however, Tabea does not share Dinah's expectations, rejecting the prospect of motherhood, all that Dinah has known for women, in favor of a life dedicated to the gods. Dinah is bewildered by her friend's hopes and knowledge: "I did not understand her desires. Indeed, I did not fully understand her words, since I knew nothing about temples or the women who serve there" (p.160). What happens to Tabea later, when Rebecca casts her out because her mother, Adath, has not performed the traditional menarche ceremony, causes Dinah intense confusion and pain. She can empathize with Tabea in a way that she could not with Ruti, and experiences her first real outburst of anger, although it is anger that she cannot fully express, certainly not to Rebecca, the object of her rage.

Dinah begins to feel a range of new emotions in this part of her story as difficult experiences compel her to grow up and think independently. Loneliness is something she has never had to suffer, so when she is left with Rebecca at Mamre, the extent of her misery is expressed in a telling simile: "I felt like a baby left outside to die" (p.190). She also begins to turn inward, keeping her thoughts and feelings to herself. She cries alone at Mamre and discovers that there are things that she may not speak. Her hatred for her grandmother is hidden, even though Rebecca is able to detect it.

She is already beginning to separate from her family but Dinah's abrupt and irreversible break with them is caused by the cataclysmic events at Shechem. Even before the murder of Shalem, Dinah has begun to transfer her loyalties to the man she feels she has married. When she wakes up to the horror of Shalem's death, she feels absolute isolation: "It seemed that I was the last person alive in the world" (p. 242). The suicidal despair that Dinah is driven to by her brothers' actions makes for change in Dinah. She is devastated by grief, but she finds a challenging adult voice through anger. Although she is still a young girl, she finds the courage to speak out against her brothers and her father with a conviction that her mothers would not be able to match; indeed, there is no evidence that Leah and Rachel say anything at all about what has happened. The force of her words takes even Dinah herself aback:

"Jacob, your sons have done murder," I said, in a voice I did not recognize as my own. "You have lied and connived, and your sons have murdered righteous men, striking them down in weakness of your own invention. You have despoiled the bodies of the dead and plundered their burying places, so their shadows will haunt you forever. You and your sons have raised up a generation of widows and orphans who will never forgive you" (p. 245).

With these words Dinah is transformed into an almost godlike agent of retribution. Renouncing her connection with the men of her family, she no longer speaks of her brothers, but "your sons"; not of her father, but "Jacob." She curses her father and brothers in the strongest possible terms. Jacob's only response is to tremble in guilt; the others are stunned into silence. Patriarchal control is here broken, Dinah's acquiescence in the decision-making of her father and brothers no longer a given. In damning her father, the highest authority in her life, and actively choosing isolation, even at the cost of losing her mothers, Dinah has to take responsibility for her own decisions.

In taking Dinah with her to Egypt, Re-nefer adopts the role of mother; however, it is clear that her motives are mixed. In part she feels to blame for Shalem's death, and so has compassion for Dinah, but the fact that Dinah will bear her grandchild carries greater weight. Both Dinah and Re-nefer find a reason to live in Re-mose.

Although she is kind to her daughter-in-law, Re-nefer is no substitute for Leah, and Dinah is thrown on her own resources in Egypt, especially after Re-mose is taken from her. Her mothers live on in her as she helps the gardeners and introduces Meryt to medicinal herbs, but she is imprisoned and isolated by her awful secret for the many years she remains voluntarily confined within Nakht-re's garden. Through love for her son, she sacrifices her own chances of a life in order to protect him from knowledge of the circumstances of his father's death. Only the persistence of Meryt draws her eventually back into the world as a midwife, but even then it is a long time before Dinah is able to break her silence. Confronted by Re-mose, who has discovered the truth about the past from Joseph, Dinah has to remember what she has suppressed and emerges from her talk with her son "broken-hearted but free" (p. 353). It marks a vital stage in Dinah's coming to terms with her own history.

Toward the end of the novel Dinah succeeds in making peace with her family, replacing anger or denial with forgiveness. When Judah gives Dinah Rachel's ring, as a gift from Leah to a daughter she never forgot, she is uncertain of its meaning but Benia interprets it as a token of Leah's forgiveness of her sister and a wish that Dinah, too, will forgive. In recalling Zilpah's words of many years before, "We are all born of the same mother" (p. 380), Dinah acknowledges her bond with her mothers and her brothers. Her final years are peaceful ones, and on her death she sees all of the women who have had a place in her life welcoming her. The last few pages of the novel are a lyrical testimony to the belief that those who are loved never die.

The emotional journey that Dinah undertakes includes only two romantic episodes. Her two marriages take place at very different stages in her life. When she meets Shalem, she is very young, having only just undergone the "opening" ceremony. Benia comes into her life when she has endured Shalem's death, the loss of her mothers and brothers, and disappointment at her distant relationship with Re-mose. In the scenes with Shalem, Diamant departs considerably from even the most liberal interpretation of Genesis 34. Far from depicting a situation leading to rape, Diamant casts Dinah's meeting with Shalem as traditional fairy-tale romance. Dinah, intrigued by a strange land, is eager to visit Shechem and the palace that Joseph has told her stories about in the same way that Cinderella longs to attend the ball. She falls in love with Shalem at first sight—"He was perfect"—but is aware that he is the king's eldest son and she merely a "hill-bred" midwife. Like Cinderella on her return from the ball, she cannot be confident that he will seek her out when she goes home after helping Ashnan in childbirth: "I thought I might never see him again. I thought perhaps it had been a mistake on my part— the fantasy of a raw country girl in the presence of a prince" (p. 219). In keeping with the conventions of romance, however, in which princes can see past superficial appearances, Shalem does not object to her dirty feet and shabby clothes. The exchanged glances, which for Dinah indicated that they had made a commitment to each other—"it was as though the bride-price had been paid and the dowry agreed to" (p. 218)—hold fast and when they next meet, their relationship is confirmed. Dinah's first sighting of Shalem when she is called back to the palace is heavily romanticized as she sees him with "sunlight filling the sky around his head like a glowing crown" (pp. 223–224).

Dinah's encounter with Shalem represents her sexual awakening. Before this moment her interest in sex has been limited to furtive gossip with Joseph and vague sensations she does not altogether understand. The physical presence of Shalem, and his difference from her brothers, stuns her. Diamant stresses the instinctive sexual responses evoked by his presence: He makes her "dumb and weak," and she discovers she is a "girl who was ready for a man" (p. 218). Unlike Cinderella in this regard, Dinah is not passive in the relationship; although her culture demands that he take the initiative in securing the relationship, there are no doubts that it is a mutual desire. Dinah is not an abused girl propelled into a sexual relationship before her time, and Shalem approaches her with proper consideration:

He looked into my face to discover my meaning, and seeing only yes, he took my hand and led me down an unfamiliar corridor into a room with a polished floor and a bed that stood on legs carved like the claws of a hawk (p. 225).

The match between Dinah and Shalem seems destined. Again reminiscent of the magic of fairy tale, the four days that they spend alone together exist almost outside time and place. The mysterious appearances of choice foods and scented baths suggest that they have a fairy-godmother watching over them, and in a way they have in Renefer. Her intervention in the romance ensures its success and conveys approval of the proposed marriage.

Dinah's time with Shalem is represented as the passion of youthful first love. Many years later, when Dinah meets Benia, there is more caution in their approach. Dinah is once again attracted immediately to the man who becomes her second husband, however, impressed by the warmth of his voice and his gentleness. As with Shalem, it takes only a look into his eyes to establish a connection between them. Though her feelings are "cooler and calmer" than those she had for Shalem, Dinah feels a sexual response to Benia at their first meeting, an "unfamiliar tightness between my legs" (p. 295); for Dinah, love and sexual feelings are inextricably linked. The initial brief exchange with Benia at the market is a prelude to a mature marriage that, once agreed, is unquestionably right. There is the same simple acceptance of each other that was evident with Shalem. When Benia comes to her two years after they first meet, Dinah has no doubts about going to the home of a man who is essentially a stranger, thinking perhaps that he has proved his worth in waiting for her. Dinah still needs a matchmaker to bring it about–Meryt replaces Re-nefer–but she finds herself with Benia in a marriage that is close to ideal with a man dissimilar in every way from those who dominated her childhood. He does not have the expectation, for example, that she will be his housekeeper: "I did not marry you to be my cook" (p. 326). Kind, thoughtful, and loving, Benia contributes to Dinah's eventual recovery from the tragedy of her youth.

In a segregated community Dinah is taught to love by women. Her earliest memories are of the loving care she receives from Leah and her other mothers. Leah tells her that at her birth they were both treated like queens in the red tent and that there "were always arms to hold you, cuddle you, embrace you" (p. 81). She learns about emotions from her mothers' stories and their interaction with her. Even sexual knowledge is imparted through their sharing of their early experiences with Jacob. The friendship she sees among the women while she is a child is maintained in her own adult life in the important relationships she has with Meryt, in particular, and with other women. Though having a husband is important at times in her life, marriage is not something Dinah seeks out. She is sustained by other women as much as by a male companion.

When Werenro performs at the banquet for Re-mose, her song has a profound effect on the audience. "The story it told was unremarkable: a tale of love found and lost—the oldest story in the world. The only story" (p. 300). Dinah's story confirms that emotional bonds are the mainstay of human life. Love sees her through—for her mothers, then Shalem and Re-mose, Meryt and Benia. Even at the end of her life she has the love of Kiya's children from whom she and Benia "received countless sweet-breathed kisses every day" (p. 382).

FEMALE EXPERIENCE

In a fictional ancient world dominated by female experience, Diamant recreates the lives of women of Mesopotamia but through a contemporary feminist perspective. She attempts to produce an authentic portrayal of women that shows the limits of their roles in 1500 B.C., but one that also highlights the responsibilities, powers, and areas of influence for which recent historical research has found evidence. In order to present a convincing female perspective, she acknowledges while at the same time moderating the extent of male dominance apparent in the stories told in Genesis. She draws on a mythology that foregrounds women's values and skills, and claims a central position for women's role in society. Incorporating some of the beliefs and challenges that contemporary feminism has asserted, she offers a reinvention of familiar characters, relationships, and situations in *The Red Tent*.

Diamant looks back to the radical feminism of the 1970s in proclaiming the value of sisterhood and foregrounding "woman-centeredness." Many radical feminists saw patriarchy (that is, a system of male domination in which women are oppressed socially and economically) as pre-eminently sexually oppressive and the prime cause of women's problems. Patriarchal oppression, they believed, ensured that female sexuality was confined by a subservience to male needs and that reproduction remained under the control of a male medical establishment. In order to break loose of such oppression, it was necessary for women to take control over their bodies and their lives. To counter male dominance radical feminists celebrated female nature and promoted the idea of sisterhood, defined by Maggie Humm as "the idea and experience of female bonding, and the self-affirmation and identity discovered in a woman-centred vision and definition of womanhood" (Humm 210–211). Sisterhood was an important concept for feminists of that time, as was the attempt to invert the assumption that male experience is paramount, women's merely secondary.

Diamant, however, by no means takes on all of the political implications of radical feminist belief; *The Red Tent* is not a utopian novel in which patriarchy is vanquished. She shows the women living within a patriarchal structure—not to do so would be to deny the reality of the context in which the novel is set—but finding or perhaps more accurately reclaiming a complementarity of gender roles. The sisters may be defined as property, handed over from one man (that is, the father) to another (that is, the husband), but within that structure they achieve control over key areas of life that might traditionally, and biologically, be perceived as women's territory. From the narrator's perspective, the world is a women's world and what is of value to women acquires universal value. In terms of sexuality, Diamant does not follow the radical feminist route from woman-centeredness into lesbianism; all her women are without doubt heterosexual. There is, however, a strong thread of sensuous eroticism in the close physical contact between the women that is perhaps more securely embedded in their daily existence than their occasional visits to Jacob's tent. The female body is represented as a potential source of liberation and power through the expression of sexual desire and the exercise of reproductive functions, and is not entirely subjected to male domination.

Foregrounding of female experience is evident from the beginning of the novel. In direct contrast to the Genesis account of Jacob and his family, the first characters the reader is introduced to in *The Red Tent* are the four sisters who share the role of Dinah's mother. Although Leah is her biological mother, each of the sisters plays her part in Dinah's development, contributing her particular skills or knowledge, and Dinah thinks of all of them as mothers. Leah, Rachel, Zilpah, and Bilhah are described in greater detail than other characters in the novel, identifying them as deserving special attention. In some ways almost a unit, they are carefully differentiated in order to make them into individuals rather than just biblical names.

Leah is maternal and closest to being the matriarch, as oldest sister and first wife. Reliable and sensible, she is the manager of the family. Diamant takes a detail from Genesis that Leah is "weak-eyed" (although it is sometimes translated as "tender-eyed") and turns it round, giving her perfect vision and strange eyes of different colors that make an impact on those she meets: "her eyes made others weak" (p.12). Leah is the earthiest of the four, associated with comfort, bread, and sex, the "lewdest of her sisters" (p. 21).

Rachel is the beautiful sister, her appearance a source of wonder to the young Dinah, who glorifies her beauty: "Rachel's presence was powerful as the moon, and just as beautiful . . . Rachel's beauty was rare and arresting" (p. 9). In the early chapters she seems selfish and demanding, trading on the effect of her physical presence. Her suffering when she fails to have a child, however, changes her and she finds her vocation in helping other women give birth. She forms the link between Inna and Dinah, passing on midwifery skills.

Zilpah is a close companion to Leah, who is of the same age. She is a clever storyteller who "used words in the most wonderful ways" (p. 15) and is primarily interested in the gods and goddesses. Unlike Leah and Rachel, she has no time for men. After giving birth to her twins, she is not called again to Jacob's tent as she makes it clear that another child would kill her. Sex with Jacob was not a pleasure, but a duty, "like grinding grain" (p. 68), to which she was resigned. Whereas Leah seems made for motherhood, Zilpah's body is not equipped for childbirth. With her endless stories of the gods and disregard for domesticity, she is seen as the eccentric sister.

The least conspicuous of the sisters is Bilhah, "tiny, dark and silent" (p.17), but kind, quietly observant, and capable of great empathy. Her ending is perhaps hinted at in the description of her as a "sad child" (p. 17). The relationship she forms with Reuben is life long; from babyhood onward she takes an interest in him and he in her. These "truest lovers" (p. 248) are destroyed by Jacob's discovery of their relationship. In the Bible there is a passing reference to Bilhah and Reuben in Genesis 35:22: "And it came to pass, when Israel dwelt in that land, that Reuben went and lay with Bilhah, his father's concubine: and Israel heard it." Diamant turns their mutual love into a tragic romance rather than leaving Bilhah as yet another fallen woman.

Each of the four mothers has different strengths. As role models they provide between them a range of qualities that can be seen as valuable in a mother, but which are rarely present in one individual.

The Meaning of the Red Tent

The withdrawal of the women into the red tent is for Dinah a matter of routine that she accepts unquestioningly as a child. No explanation is given for the tent's existence, but the reader is made aware of its value to Dinah's mothers as a place where they are able to relax together, temporarily free of their domestic duties. Leah reveals the full significance of the red tent to Dinah only at Mamre, after Rebecca has banished Tabea. In a compelling speech she shows how the tent is somewhere that women can claim as a space of their own, set apart from men, its secrets unknown to them: "In the red tent, the truth is known" (p.188). Leah emphasizes the importance of a tradition that has passed down from "our mothers and their mothers"; it provides a key link between women, and gives menstruation its place at the source of life. Innana "gave a gift to women that is not known among men, and this is the secret of blood" (p.187). (Innana, the Queen of Heaven, was a fertility goddess.) The red tent thus becomes a strong symbol of female solidarity and an assertion of women's power as the bringers of life. Menstruation is not regarded in the novel as a problem or a curse; rather, it is almost a blessing, with sacred rituals handed down from women to their daughters. Both menstruation and childbirth are the province of women, who help and support one another. The women feel in tune with the world as they menstruate in accordance with the lunar cycle and in synchronicity with one another, as has been shown to be common for women who live in close proximity. They all begin to menstruate when the sun sets on the new moon. The color red suggests not only blood, but passion and power, and renders the tent an assertive presence. Rather than retreating in shame to a remote place, the women enter the tent with pride.

The celebratory attitude toward menstruation and its rituals is shown in the novel to be under threat. Women who join Jacob's tribe from other communities are ignorant of the ceremonies or suspicious of them. A crisis occurs when Dinah reaches the menarche. She is pleased at her entry into womanhood and looks forward to being initiated into the secrets of adult life. Her opening ceremony is a time of pleasure and happiness. Levi's wife, Inbu, however, is shocked by the ritual and tells her husband, who informs Jacob of "abominations" (p. 207). Inbu breaks the implicit alliance among the women to protect their ceremonies and their gods, and thus puts their continuance at risk. Jacob, who has been content previously to live in ignorance of his wives' activities in the red tent, has to acknowledge that they are still worshipping their household gods and is driven to destroy them. "And Jacob began to frown at the red tent" (p. 208).

There is no historical evidence for the existence of a red tent as Diamant uses it in the novel; however, separation rituals for menstruation exist in many cultures. Menstrual huts are certainly common, in which girls on puberty would retreat from the light, often forbidden to touch water or the earth. (The latter is referred to in the novel on p. 208 when Dinah learns how to keep her feet from touching bare earth.) Some of the rituals are celebratory in nature, identifying women's connection with the earth and the spirit world; however, menstruation is often taboo, an unclean bodily function that necessitates ostracism and is viewed with fear. Women in such cultures are kept in isolation, away from the community and without the support of other women. Judy Grahn shows how menstruation has been regarded as dangerous by some people; the breaking of taboo was believed to bring harm to the menstruating woman and to others:

If she failed to keep her taboos, her community would no longer thrive. Thus, she could not look at the sky or the planets. Nor could she gaze at bodies of water, for fear of causing a flood; if she were to look at trees and plants, they would wither. She had to protect the sources of water, so she could not look at the pond, or it would dry up (Grahn, p. 18).

Such excessive and irrational fears of the destructive potential of menstruation are an acknowledgment of the power inherent in women's association with blood and birth, even though that power has frequently been denied them or turned against them in patriarchal societies.

The idea that menstruation is dangerous, or at least unmentionable, is the one that has largely prevailed, certainly in Western culture. Victorian medicine tended to approach menstruation, and any female reproductive function, with extreme wariness. An association was often made between menstruation and insanity: "Menarche was the first stage of mental danger, requiring anxious supervision from mothers if daughters were to emerge unscathed" (Showalter, *Female Malady*, p. 56). The fact that menstruation is tied to the lunar cycle is supposed to link women to the capricious machinery of the planets.

Jordan Paper, in his book *Through the Earth Darkly* (1997), which considers female spirituality in various early cultures including the developing Israelite religion, discusses observances of menstruation that regard it as a sacred blessing. He points out that in such cultures "women in general have a strong sense of identity and self-worth as females . . . in cultures where menstruation is celebrated and the power of menstrual blood overtly acknowledged, women have a sure sense of their own power" (pp. 244–245). This is borne out in *The Red Tent* where Leah and her sisters are certain of their role and their value in the family. Even in such a heavily patriarchal context, women have a complementary not a subsidiary function to men.

Diamant's choice of positive historical readings of menstruation makes the red tent a focal point of the first part of the novel; however, because its existence is shown as under threat, there is a strong suggestion that this idyll of female community may not last much longer. When Dinah moves far away from her place of birth, the red tent ceases to be relevant.

Female Friendship and Sisterhood

The primacy of female friendship in Dinah's childhood community is well established in the novel. Although there are conflicts between the sisters, and with other women, the achievement of contentment in life largely depends on the maintenance of strong female bonds. For Dinah it is her mothers, later Meryt and, to a much lesser extent, Re-nefer, who enable her to be strong enough to survive and flourish.

Diamant does not give a sentimental view of sisterhood. The bonds that hold the women together are based on an understanding of mutual self-interest and a tolerance of differences. The sisters and the bondswomen take pleasure in one another's company—there is plenty of laughter in Dinah's childhood—but negative feelings are always present. Zilpah is not fond of Rachel and is largely responsible for Rachel's fear of her wedding night, her imagination stirred by Zilpah's malicious accounts of Jacob's likely sexual demands. The sisters are often critical of one another, but the relationship between Leah and Rachel shows that, when it matters, the women are united.

Leah and Rachel, bound to share a husband, inevitably feel resentment of each other—Rachel because Leah is the head wife and Leah because Rachel is the preferred one. The jealousy between them lasts for many years until they reach peace and finally friendship. The unease prompted by their situation is always transcended when it is necessary for the women to act together to support, protect, or honor their kind. They maintain a solidarity that gives them power. The move to Canaan is a major event in the sisters' lives. In Part Two, Chapter Two, while Jacob is planning the journey, the four women talk among themselves in the red tent, and each of them voices her views in an orderly and democratic way. Each has her say, they air their disagreements, and finally come to the bold conclusion that they are prepared to go, but will take with them the household gods, the teraphim. Although they may in reality have no choice about going with Jacob, it is important that the sisters reach their own judgment, and it is only after they have discussed it fully that Leah approaches Jacob to say that his wives are ready to accompany him. Dinah witnesses the scene and is surprised to see that "[b]y her side was Rachel" (p. 109). Whatever coolness may exist between the sisters, they are together with Jacob on this occasion "talking like old friends."

At important moments in life, notably births and deaths, all of the women join to mark the occasion. Part One, Chapter Two, deals with Reuben's birth and Adah's death. Leah is "pampered by her sisters, who barely let her feet touch the earth" (p. 52), and Adah shares in the joy brought by her daughter's child. Adah dies shortly thereafter, and she receives all of the women's attention: "[T]hey put ashes in their hair and honored her" (p. 53).

The confidence that this supportive framework gives the sisters allows them to speak out for women outside of their close group. Interventions are made on behalf of both Inna and Ruti, both of whom were unprotected, for different reasons, by a family group. Inna's vulnerability is produced by her unmarried state. Living alone since her mother's death, she has no family to turn to when she is involved in an angry dispute with a stranger. His accusation that "[a] woman alone is a danger" (p. 128) reflects the age-old suspicion of spinsters. When he says, "Where are your judges? . . . Who are your elders?", he highlights society's fear of the independent woman, uncontrolled by male family members. Rachel is able to appeal for her with Jacob and the first word she speaks to Inna after Jacob has given his assent is "sister," recognizing her friend's place in their group.

The treatment of Ruti seems to exhibit quite the reverse of sisterhood. As Laban's last wife and mother of his two sons, she might be expected to have the sisters' support; however, they ignore and distrust her. In terms of status, she is lowly, bought more or less as a slave rather than negotiated for as a dowered bride. Laban buys her for sexual services and mistreats her constantly after briefly rewarding her for giving him sons. Ruti is rarely mentioned and her name is usually prefaced in Dinah's narrative with the epithet "poor," showing at least awareness of Ruti's situation. The sisters feel pity for her, but it is tempered by the knowledge that her sons are rivals to theirs. They allow her to become a victim, virtually invisible in the camp, "such a ragged, battered misery to look at that no one saw her" (p. 75). In the end the sisters help Ruti, first by aborting the child she does not want and, more significantly, by pleading with Jacob to redeem her from slavery after Laban gambles her away. Leah's action in persuading Jacob to buy Ruti back is courageous and she receives inordinate gratitude from Ruti in return, but their support for her is too late and too little. She is abused by Laban more than ever after Jacob's intervention, and dies a sad and lonely death. Ruti's fate perhaps shows the limits of sisterhood within a patriarchal structure. Although they might have prevented Ruti's isolation, and overcome their anxieties about the future of their own sons, they could not have stopped the bullying by Laban and Ruti's sons. The sisters are fortunate to have in Jacob a husband who is considerate and kind; but it might not have been so.

The fellowship among the sisters may in some ways be democratic, but there is an implicit acceptance of hierarchy. All women are not equal. Even among the sisters, the inferior status of Zilpah and Bilhah is acknowledged on numerous occasions, although it does not affect the relationship between them. The bondswomen, who are not generally named individually, are of lower status than any of the sisters. They are treated with respect and enter the red tent with the sisters (a day later), but there is no questioning of their position.

Despite the inevitable limitations of sisterhood in this context, the period spent in Haran exists in the novel as a kind of golden age for female friendship. The last time that the women meet in the red tent before leaving for Canaan is described as "more like a funeral than a feast" (p. 115). Only two of the bondswomen will be joining Jacob's group and there is a sense that the camaraderie achieved in the red tent will be lost:

It was the end of a long sisterhood. They had held one another's legs in childbirth and suckled one another's babies. They had laughed in the garden and sung harmonies for the new moon. But those days were ending and each woman sat with her own memories, her own loss (p.115).

Dinah's later experience does not replicate the ideal of the red tent. Her most enduring support comes from Meryt, who becomes mother, sister, colleague, and friend. The friendship is deep, as is revealed by Dinah's heartbroken response to her death, but a friendship between two individuals, even such a perfect one as this, does not offer the supportive environment available to Dinah's mothers. Dinah's life in Egypt, as the sole wife of a working man, with a close female companion and a job of her own, seems more akin to a modern way of living while the sisterhood in Haran belongs to a lost past.

Sexuality

Friendship between women in Part One of the novel finds physical as much as verbal expression. They help with their hands in childbirth, they bathe and massage the sick, and they freely display physical affection. At times their intimacy takes on an erotic quality, as at Dinah's opening ceremony. The mothers do everything they can to bring Dinah pleasure and relaxation: "They would not let me feed myself, but used their fingers to fill my mouth with the choicest morsels. They massaged my neck and back until I was as supple as a cat" (p. 204). They sing her songs and give her plenty of wine. It is a serious but joyous occasion in which all the women participate. For the ceremony itself, in which Dinah's hymen is broken by the frog-shaped figure, her four mothers gather around her and she is "in love with them all" (p. 206). The act of penetration by the "little goddess" is a sexual initiation. Dinah feels like a "slip of cloth" caught between the Queen (Innana) and her consort making love, and she is "warmed by the great passion." The sympathetic moaning by the mothers suggests a shared sexual experience. This method of introduction to adult sexuality is an entirely female affair and takes the right to an untouched bride away from any future husband. The mothers' way is explicitly contrasted to a ritual more commonly known in which the bloody bedding of a bride is publicly displayed after her wedding night as proof of her virginity. This, the tradition accepted by the Canaanite women, is represented by Dinah as something rather distasteful: "As though my father would wish to look upon a woman's blood" (p. 207).

Within the limits of a polygamous marriage, in a culture that denies women power, the sisters are able to exercise some choice in their sexual activity. Although being called to one's husband's tent at whim may seem to deny consent, there is no suggestion that Jacob's wives are forced into unwanted sex. Diamant stresses Jacob's considerate approaches to his wives, seeking to give them pleasure rather than imposing himself on them. For example, he makes a particular effort to win over Zilpah, who is the most reluctant of the four. Apart from Zilpah, all of the sisters enjoy their sexual experiences. It takes some time for Rachel because of her initial anxiety and her inability to maintain a pregnancy; but she discovers her sexuality when Bilpah has a child for her: "After all the years, all the nights, all the miscarriages and broken hopes, Rachel found delight in his arms" (p. 66). Female sexuality is represented in the novel as something to be explored and relished. When Leah and Bilhah return to their sisters after sleeping with Jacob for the first time, they are eager to tell all, allowing the others vicarious pleasure. Leah's time with Jacob after their wedding is described as a "golden week" in which Leah finds powerful sexual feelings. From first meeting Jacob, Leah has been in love with him and her desire is freely expressed; however, there is not an insistence in the novel that all women should be sexual, but that, as in other aspects of female life, choice and the acceptance of difference are what matters. Those who find fulfilment in sex, especially Leah and Dinah, are able to enjoy it; others, like Zilpah, seek pleasure in other activities.

Maternity and Motherhood

When Bilhah suggests to Rachel that she could have a child for her, she has a longing both to experience sex and to "become part of the great mother-mystery" (p. 61). Most of the women in the novel see motherhood as an essential part of female life. Leah gives birth to Reuben "eager to be admitted to the sisterhood of mothers" (p. 46). To bear a child in this community has obvious benefits in terms of ensuring the position of the mother; producing a son confers special status. It is the physical experience itself, however, and the entry into a shared female mystery, that really counts for the women in Dinah's family. Dinah's one experience of birth is an initiation into adulthood and allows her to see her place in the cycles of life and death:

Like every mother since the first mother, I was overcome and bereft, exalted and ravaged. I had crossed over from girlhood. I beheld myself as an infant in my mother's arms, and caught a glimpse of my own death (p. 270).

Not all contemporary female writers have been so unambivalent about motherhood, but Diamant upholds the belief that the ability to give birth is what defines womanhood; however, she does not discount the possibility of opting out. The novel avoids endorsing traditional notions of "maternal instinct" that have coerced women into thinking themselves unnatural if they do not wish to, or are unable to, become mothers. Zilpah likes the idea of a daughter to teach, but she does not choose to risk a second pregnancy to have one. Tabea is not interested in having children, "not willing to suffer" the pain and sometimes death she has witnessed in her family (p.159). Meryt is unable to have a child (p. 283), but she is treated with respect and affection by her adopted sons and supports other mothers through midwifery.

Becoming a mother is a biological process. The physical changes of pregnancy and the stresses of birth are detailed in the novel on many occasions, showing both the similarities and the differences in women's experiences. Thus, Leah has a straightforward first birth, as does Bilhah, but it is much more difficult for Zilpah, with her narrow hips unsuited to childbirth, as she strains for three days and comes close to death. The hazards of childbirth without the aid of modern medicine and, crucially, blood transfusions are not minimized. Rachel suffers badly in giving birth to Joseph and dies in agony having Benjamin. Even with the help of experienced midwives, some women die in childbirth, often through uncontrollable blood loss, or their babies are stillborn. A particularly harrowing account is of Hatnuf, Ruddedit's daughter, who is already "nearly dead with fear and pain" (p.286) when Dinah and Meryt arrive to help her. All of their efforts serve to save only one of the babies she was carrying, and Hatnuf herself dies from the "torrent of blood" that accompanies his arrival.

Being a mother is not entirely down to biology. Diamant also shows social aspects of mothering in the novel. Once a child is born in Jacob's camp, the baby is not regarded as the sole responsibility of his or her biological mother. All of the women handle the child and, as has been the norm in the past, others will feed a baby if the mother cannot. Rachel is unable to feed Joseph, so Leah feeds him along with Dinah (p. 85). The bond between mother and child is important, but it is not sacrosanct. This becomes more evident with the older children, who tend to seek out the mother who best suits them. Reuben is Leah's child, but clings to Bilhah; Gad and Asher, who do not really understand the oddities of their own mother, Zilpah, turn to Leah, who makes much better bread. The mothers do not resent these changes of allegiance because everyone receives a share of the attention in a growing community. When Tali and Issa, Leah's twins, seek out other mothers, Leah tries to bribe them back, but is too busy to make great efforts to hold on to her sons: "And she did not suffer for lack of love" (p. 98).

The major beneficiary of this communal method of childrearing, of course, is Dinah, who always has one of her mothers to turn to for help and consolation. Their methods allow the children to be nurtured without risking a possibly unhealthy symbiotic relationship developing between mother and child. There is benefit also for the mothers who are not confined by childrearing, but who can have an identity that is not just that of mother. It is different for Dinah, who is isolated in her mothering. As she goes into labor, she cries out for the mothers who are not there to help her, "feeling the absence of four beloved faces, four pairs of tender hands" (p. 266). During the years in which Dinah has charge of her son, there is less integration of young children into the family than Dinah has been used to; she and Re-mose are sent from the house into the garden "where his mess did not soil the floors and where his prattle would not disturb the work of the scribes" (p. 274).

Dinah's experience in Egypt reveals an aspect of mothering less acceptable both for her and for the modern reader. She loses her son after only a few years although it is made clear to her from birth that Re-mose, whose name she has not even chosen, does not belong to her. On waking after his birth, she finds her baby gone, only to be told that he is "with his mother" (p. 270). Dinah is confused and Meryt has to tell her gently that the "mother" is Re-nefer. Re-nefer makes it plain to Dinah that she may be her son's biological mother, but in every other way he belongs to Nakht-re's family. His future is determined by his uncle, his place in the world of men set out for him. In terms of control, Dinah has none as his mother, whereas his uncle takes the place of his dead father as patriarch.

In *Of Mother Born*, Adrienne Rich makes a distinction between the experience of pregnancy and birth and the institution of mother-hood. She defines two meanings of *motherhood*: "[T]he *potential relationship* of any woman to her powers of reproduction and to children; and the *institution*, which aims at ensuring that that potential—and all women—, shall remain under male control" (p.13). The distinction she makes concerns power. Either women themselves decide how, when, and whether they mother, or men make those decisions for them as, she claims, is most often the case. In the first part of *The Red Tent* the women work together to have some degree of control over mothering, so male decision making in child-rearing is much less apparent in Haran than it is in Egypt. When Dinah becomes a mother, she has no power and no choice but to comply with decisions made by Nakht-re.

Four of the female characters in the novel—Inna, Rachel, Dinah, and Meryt—are midwives. Although they have limited personal experience of childbirth between them—two of them have never had a child—their contribution to the well being of other women is invaluable. Their skills are extensive, stretching beyond aiding childbirth into other aspects of medicine. On many occasions the midwife is the nearest to a doctor that anyone has. The midwife's kit, the ancient equivalent of a doctor's bag, is a cherished object. On page 47 Inna produces the equipment from hers that she needs for helping Leah, "[t]he knife, the string, reeds for suction, amphorae of cumin, hyssop, and mint oil," plus the two bricks on which the women stand to give birth in an upright position. Later in the novel, when Dinah has become a celebrated midwife, Benia makes her, as a present when she first becomes his wife, a beautiful box to hold her midwifery equipment. It is made of ebony, "wood that was used almost exclusively for the tombs of kings" (p. 325), suggesting both Benia's love for Dinah and the respect he extends to her work.

Midwives have a wealth of medical knowledge that enables them to deal with a range of ailments and problems. They have herbal remedies for wounds and fever, and soporifics to bring sleep and relieve pain. Inna gives Rachel treatments to encourage conception from her "seemingly endless list of concoctions and strategies" (p. 56), but also helps with contraception when the time does not seem right for another pregnancy. Rachel even helps Ruti with an abortion when she cannot endure the prospect of giving Laban another child. It has to be done in absolute secrecy, but Rachel is confident that the men have no idea of what the women know and do.

The female practice of medicine that is shown in the novel is characterized by its competence, its inclusiveness, and its humanity. Childbirth is not a clinical procedure; rather, it is an occasion for the women to work together for a common purpose. Inna talks constantly at the birth of Reuben, "banishing the frightened silence that had made a wall around Leah" (p. 47), and gives support with encouraging words and physical contact. Women without midwifery skills can also take part in the process: Zilpah and Dinah form Leah's chair as she prepares to push. Song is used to relax the laboring mother. In Shechem, Inna and Rachel learn a new birth song from the women there that proves to be "the most soothing balm that Inna and Rachel had ever used" (p. 210). This powerful song is the one that Dinah sings to Meryt as she drifts into death, drawing together the start and end of life in an appropriate way for a woman who has spent most of her life bringing babies into the world.

Midwifery is practiced in a spirit of co-operation and generosity. Women share knowledge and are prepared to be corrected in their methods if they can improve their abilities. Meryt learns from Dinah about new herbs as well as the technique of episiotomy, which she tries in a desperate moment, at Dinah's request, when Re-mose is struggling to be born. Men play no visible role in childbirth; male medical practitioners are rarely mentioned at all while Dinah is in Egypt, and their usefulness is doubted. Re-nefer suggests calling for a surgeon when Dinah is in difficulties, but Meryt, who was sent to train as a midwife because she was reckoned clever, manages to save the baby without help. Dinah is called by Joseph to attend As-naat after the "physicians and necromancers have done her no good" (p. 335). When Hatnuf is in great pain, the "physician-priest" actually increases her suffering by smoking goat-dung in the room, which causes Hatnuf to faint and injure herself. Male control of reproduction, through the replacement of midwives with male obstetricians, and the medicalization of childbirth, which has been a cause of conflict in more recent times, are avoided in the novel. Birth belongs to the women.

Women's Work and Roles in the Family

In Haran the work of women is vital to the family. Before Jacob's arrival, Laban's household has been in decline. Leah's efforts have ensured the family's survival. In the absence of sons, Rachel has helped with the flock, but Leah has been the family's manager. Jacob quickly learns that it is she to whom he should go for advice or information. Leah's main duties are cooking and brewing, but she is involved also in decisions that would normally be left to the men. She knows which traders are reliable and which boys should be hired at shearing time; she memorizes details about the flock that Bilhah has observed. Jacob's dependence on Leah persists. Although Leah is careful not to assume it, she is often effectively in charge. When they are about to leave for Canaan, Leah gently advises her husband on arrangements for packing up, and Rachel suggests when it is time to leave: "My husband may know better, but the herds are ready and the goods are packed. Our feet are shod and we stand with nothing to do" (p.123). Without exceeding their roles and being careful to maintain due deference, Leah, and, to a lesser extent, Rachel run the household.

Jacob's wives all engage in traditional female domestic tasks: cooking, spinning, weaving, gardening, and brewing. Brewing beer was exclusively women's work at that time). This work is seen as equal in value to the work of the men with the flocks or in the fields. Their skills ensure that the family is clothed and fed. The women make their contribution economically through the goods they produce for trade. It is explicitly stated that Jacob's work alone would not have brought the family the prosperity they achieved:

The family's good fortune and increasing wealth were not entirely the result of Jacob's skill, nor could it all be attributed to the will of the gods. My mothers' labors accounted for much of it. While sheep and goats are a sign of wealth, their full value is realized only in the husbandry of women. Leah's cheeses never soured, and when the rust attacked wheat or millet, she saw to it that the afflicted stems were picked clean to protect the rest of the crop. Zilpah and Bilhah wove the wool from Jacob's growing flocks into patterns of black, white, and saffron that lured traders and brought new wealth (p. 54).

Women's work is not represented as mundane. The sisters take great pride in what they do—Leah in her cooking, Bilhah in her spinning and weaving—and Dinah comes to appreciate the artistry of their accomplishments when she learns from them the "alchemy" of baking and brewing, and struggles to master weaving. The valuable craftsmanship of weaving is illustrated in the story of Uttu, which Bilhah tells Dinah as she is teaching her to spin (pp. 94–95). In the story Uttu, the goddess of weaving, also the deity of plants, wishes to teach spinning and weaving to mortal women to give them a means of protection from the elements. Her father thinks that the women will be too stupid to grasp the intricacies of the craft, but when Uttu finds a woman, Enhenduanna, willing to learn, a transformation takes place. The women learn the arts and cookery; their lives are changed. The implication is that spinning and weaving are associated with civilization and progress.

In Egypt Dinah lives a life too isolated to have much awareness of the work of women, but she does notice a difference in relationships between the sexes. Used to a culture in which men and women exist in separate spheres, she is surprised at the first banquet given for Remose where husbands and wives sit together to eat and touch each other in public. She knows little of what women do, however, and realizes at Re-nefer's death that she is ignorant of how her mother-in-law "kept busy"; in this wealthy and leisured household, she would not be required to do any work.

Female Wisdom and Worship

In the earlier parts of the novel the women are sustained by the worship of an array of ancient Mesopotamian gods and goddesses. There were hundreds of such deities, who were deemed responsible for all aspects of the human and natural world. Although many are referred to, the most important goddesses for the sisters are Innana, the Queen of Heaven, later known as Ishtar, and Anath, often fused with Asherah and Astarte. Dedication to the goddesses is part of their daily lives, seen in such rituals as the baking of bread for Innana on the seventh day (which Rebecca also does) and calling on them for help during childbirth and at other difficult times. In addition to expressing devotion to the major goddesses, each sister has her personal favorite, connected in some way with her interests or personality. Zilpah reveals her special deity, normally kept secret until near death, when the sisters are contemplating departure for Canaan. Her goddess is Nanshe (responsible for dreams and singers), whereas Rachel favors Gula (goddess of healing), Bilhah Uttu (the weaver), and Leah Ninkasi (the brewer of beer). The strength of feeling about the goddesses is apparent in the decision to take the teraphim with them, stealing them from Laban. Although the sisters are realistic about the limits of the powers of the gods, with Leah especially showing skepticism, there is a sense that the goddesses bring hope. As Rachel says, "'I know that women in travail find strength and comfort in the names of their gods. I have seen them struggle beyond all hope at the sound of an incantation. I have seen life spared at the last moment, for no other reason than that hope" (p.107).

The presence in their lives of these goddesses is also a reminder of female power. In their sphere the goddesses had enormous power.

Innana (*Nin-an-na*, "Lady of Sky"), the Queen of Heaven and Earth, was probably the most influential deity of the ancient world; the much venerated universal goddess of ancient Sumer/Mesopotamia. Even though she was originally a fertility goddess, she increased her influence. According to Jordan Paper, even kings looked to her:

In Sumer, the power of the male kingship appears to have been entirely dependent on Innana. . . . The justification for kingship was the king's satisfying Inanna so that she would continue to assure the fertility and safety of the land. The mythic early material of Mesopotamia repeatedly insists that no king could reign without Innana's approval (Paper 33).

Anath, goddess of love and war, also displayed considerable powers that are not conventionally feminine. She was sexually aggressive and bloodthirsty, a warlike deity fighting many battles, although Diamant foregrounds her role as healer and defender of mothers. Asherah, who is sometimes seen as consort for El, or Yahweh, was a popular and common Canaanite goddess, the original bread of life. Women molded loaves of the figure of Asherah that were then ritually eaten. Idols representing Asherah were placed under trees or erected as poles and pillars, as is demonstrated in the novel. These powerful, sexual, often frightening figures are a demonstration of female dominance or, at the very least, equality.

Diamant highlights most the consolatory aspects of the goddesses—their support to the women—and makes a stark contrast with Jacob's god, El. Zilpah, the sister who most relies on the goddesses, is not impressed with Jacob's god. He is for her a "hard, strange god, alien and cold" (p.15), although, she acknowledges, perhaps worthy to be consort of Innana. El seems a remote god. whereas the many goddesses of the sisters have been domesticated to a degree, providing inspiration and comfort.

In Egypt Dinah makes fewer mentions of the old goddesses, and only passing reference to such Egyptian gods as Osiris (ruler of the underworld and god of vegetation) and the Golden Lady Hathor (goddess of love, beauty, and music, but also of such other things as women, fertility, and childbirth); however, Dinah's childhood beliefs and observances stay with her.

The power attributed to the goddesses is communicated to the women through the skills they acquire—their excellence at weaving, medicine, brewing, and cultivation—and in various inexplicable ways. Rachel is connected right from the start with water, without which survival would be impossible. Diamant does not make her a "water witch" (p.10), as her family had hoped she would be, but the scent of water that hangs about her, "the smell of life and wealth," suggests that she is obscurely responsible for the well that ensures their existence. The knowledge and the wisdom that the sisters display and teach to Dinah is a female legacy that assures prosperity and the continuance of female mastery. After Meryt's death, Dinah becomes the oldest of her adopted family and takes on the mantle of matriarch, which others have had before her. Leah says to Dinah in a dream, "[Y]ou are the grandmother, giving voice to wisdom" (pp. 359–360), and Dinah realizes that she is the "wise woman, the mother, grandmother, and even great-grandmother," passing on knowledge in her turn.

The most powerful matriarchal figure in the novel is Rebecca, known to Dinah as "the grandmother." The use of the definite article *the* reinforces her status in the family (Isaac seems almost inconsequential), but additionally establishes her as the Grand Mother, embodiment of female authority. Living as a priestess, she is an awesome figure who almost achieves the stature of a goddess. There is historical evidence of female priests at this time, usually living a life of chastity, with the most important, the *entu*, acting as a female deity on earth, an incarnation of Innana (Paper 36). Dressed in regal purple and occupying a magnificent tent that looks like an "earthbound rainbow," Rebecca has virtually freed herself from patriarchal control. Isaac lives apart from her, she is served only by women (that is, the Deborahs) and does not serve men, as women generally do. Dinah does not perceive Rebecca so much as a relative, but as a "force of the gods." She is a distant figure who seems to have transcended ordinary emotional bonds to act as dispassionate judge. Her cursing of Adath for failing to carry out the ceremony for Tabea is done in a fury worthy of the gods. Her energy and drive mark her as an exceptional being, who, Dinah thinks, "seemed to burn with some kind of fire" (p. 191).

Rebecca sees herself as the end of the line, with no apparent inheritor of her position. As elsewhere in the novel, traditions of female authority are shown to be in decline. In this context Rebecca's treatment of Tabea, which seems so shocking and incomprehensible to Dinah and probably to many readers, has some justification. The rituals and practices that have sustained Dinah's mothers and brought them contentment and control are at risk, and Rebecca attempts to preserve them, even if it is at the expense of the future of a young girl. By the end of Dinah's visit, however, Rebecca seems to have given up hope for the future when she says, "Mamre will be forgotten. The tent will not stand after me" (p.198).

The representation of women and their experiences in *The Red Tent* is fundamentally a confirmation of an essentialist view of gender; that is, the idea that there is a female nature innate in all women. Although Diamant offers a broad and generous view of what constitutes womanhood, she accepts the belief that there is common ground to be shared by women, regardless of their class or race or individual differences. In highlighting traditional female concerns with the domestic—the bringing up of children and management of households—and revitalizing women's ancient connections with sources of power, she gives what is essentially *female* a restored value. She does not, however, show women succeeding in male spheres or transcending the definitions of femininity to redefine understanding of what it means to be female.

The Novel's Reception

It is not uncommon for journalists to turn to writing novels and to become successful at it, particularly within popular fiction. In the 1990s Nicci Gerrard of the *Observer* (United Kingdom) developed a flourishing second career writing thrillers with her husband, Sean French. Carl Hiaasen, who has produced a series of very popular comic crime novels, is also employed by the *Miami Herald*. A late start, although it can be a disadvantage in a culture obsessed with youthful authors whose attractive faces can adorn publicity material, does not preclude the possibility of writing a best seller. In Diamant's case, however, publishing her first novel in her mid-forties made it first seem that her venture into a different kind of writing would remain little more than a hobby. Although she was already a published writer, the majority of her journalism appeared in newspapers within the Boston area, and her "Life Cycle" books on Jewish life attracted a limited, specialized readership. Even though known, her name would not in itself guarantee attention in a new literary context.

Diamant completed *The Red Tent* without having found a publisher. She saw the writing more as a challenge to herself than as a means of enhancing her reputation or earning a fortune: "I had no deadline, no contract, no financial incentive. It was the most open-ended thing I'd ever written, both liberating and daunting" (Musleah). She initially had difficulty even finding an agent to take it. Those she thought would appreciate it did not, and when she sent it to some agents she knew, only one was interested, and he had to back out because of other commitments. She eventually found an agent locally that sent it to five publishers, one of who, St. Martin's Press, took on the title. She sold the manuscript for a small advance. Problems continued, however, even at the time of publication. When it was first released in October 1997, the novel was not advertised; Diamant's editor had been fired a month before the book came out, and the new editor did not have the time to promote it. As Diamant said in an interview with Faith L. Justice, it "became an orphan book." The novel received no reviews in major publications and Diamant suggested in her interview with Justice that her education and contacts were simply not prestigious enough to ensure exposure in the newspapers and magazines that have influence:

I'm not a literary writer. I didn't go to whatever school it is or have the mentor you need to get reviewed in the *New York Times*. Publishing is a weird business. There are good books that don't get published and crappy books that get published and promoted up the wazoo. It seems pretty serendipitous and arbitrary to me. I had luck in that I found an agent, a publisher liked the book, and published it beautifully.

With no publicity and few reviews, *The Red Tent* achieved modest sales in hardcover of slightly more than 10,000 copies. Those reviews that did appear at the time of first publication were generally appreciative, but they did not quite foresee the broad appeal and enormous following the novel would have within a couple of years. *Kirkus Reviews*, which provides prepublication reviews, described it on September 15, 1997, as "[c]ubits beyond most Woman-of-the-Bible sagas in sweep and vigor," a "readable tale" with "stirring scenery and a narrative of force and color." The reviewer's final comment, however, categorized it as a novel of interest only to a particular readership: "For a liberal Bible audience." Its selection for review by the *Christian Science Monitor* also indicated that *The Red Tent* might not be a novel that would find favor with a wide-ranging readership. In the January 27, 1998, edition the reviewer, Merle Rubin, included *The Red Tent* in an article on first novels as one of four that had "managed to hold my attention" and "engage my imagination." Although she classified it as a "biblical novel," Rubin commented on the "inventiveness" of the "compelling" tale and in identifying its "timeless resonance," perhaps recognized some of the qualities that later were to draw in hundreds of thousands of readers. Those readers were certainly not to be found in 1997:

When Anita Diamant went to Los Angeles to do a reading and book signing for her novel, *The Red Tent*, only her best friend from junior high school and her friend's mom showed up. Nobody came to her next reading. "It was painful," Diamant recalls with a wince (English).

4

The Novel's Performance

After an unpromising start, *The Red Tent* went on to become what is consistently referred to as a "word-of-mouth publishing phenomenon." Even though it was never acknowledged by the major reviewing publications, the novel achieved bestseller status, remaining in national book charts consistently throughout 2001 and 2002. In marked contrast to her earlier disheartening experience at book signings, Diamant did a reading in Detroit in December 1999 that was attended by more than 900 people. In early 2000 the novel merited a full-page advertisement in the *New York Times Book Review*; Diamant surmizes that the cost was probably greater than her advance from St. Martin's Press (English).

The extraordinary success of *The Red Tent* is in part the result of some shrewd promotion by both Diamant herself, who devoted three years to publicizing it, and her paperback editor; however, it might have more to do with its remarkable appeal to legions of readers, especially women, who bought the novel and passed it on to friends and family, or recommended it at meetings of book groups. This kind of success is relatively unusual in publishing, although another notable example is Rebecca Wells' *Divine Secrets of the Ya-Ya*

Sisterhood, which occupies a similar place in the minds of the female reading public. Wells, like Diamant, made great personal efforts to promote her novel.

After respectable but not spectacular sales, St. Martin's Press was considering remaindering its unsold hardcovers within a year of the publication of *The Red Tent*. Diamant herself argued that the books could be used more profitably for promotion. A direct approach to the Jewish community, in which she already played an active role, proved immensely worthwhile. *The Red Tent* was sent first to 500 female rabbis in Reform Judaism; Diamant knew the president of the organization who wrote a covering letter. Another friend, president of the Reconstructionist Rabbinic Assembly, also endorsed the book, and copies were sent to both male and female rabbis. Through preaching and direct recommendation, readers came to hear of the book. Because of the nature of the novel and Diamant's position as someone who had already been writing for and about the Jewish community for a decade, it was received enthusiastically.

Perhaps the biggest break at this time came with its exposure in the *Reform Judaism Magazine*, which has a circulation of about 400,000. In its Summer 1999 edition, *The Red Tent* was named as a "significant Jewish book." In each issue, the magazine recommends two titles "representing the best of Jewish literature, both fiction and nonfiction," and encourages readers to read the chosen texts on their own or in the book groups that are a feature of Jewish culture. The reviewer, Bonny V. Fetterman, considered the novel in terms of its reinterpretation of biblical narrative and included an extract from the Prologue: "Unlike the biblical narrative, which depicts her solely as a victim and a pawn, Diamant's *midrash* portrays Dinah as a woman with a will of her own." In addition to the review, the magazine has produced a study guide to the novel that can be found on their website. Diamant commented on the feature:

That's a recommendation with a lot of impact. November is Jewish book month, so Jewish Community Centers all around the country have book fairs where they invite authors and sell books in advance of the holidays. I had done that with my other books. I only had a little interest in *The Red Tent* the second year it was out, but the next year, I had to turn down invitations to speak all over the country (Justice).

Diamant also proved to be fortunate in her paperback editor, Diane Higgins, who was keen to market the novel. Picador, the paperback division of St. Martin's, brought out *The Red Tent* in November 1998. In addition to the mailings to the Jewish community, Picador offered copies of the novel to independent reading group leaders and female Christian clergy (325 to Protestant ministers and 100 to nuns and priests). They targeted reading groups by offering discounts if bookshops bought ten or more copies. With reading groups very much in mind, Picador has its own reading guide to the novel on its website. Books were sent also to such major booksellers as Barnes and Noble and Borders although Diamant gives credit more to the smaller independent booksellers who made personal recommendations of the novel to their customers. The independents "know their readers and they know what they like and support those books"; they "hand sell" (Justice). In 2001, the independent booksellers alliance, Book Sense, made *The Red Tent* its Book of the Year.

Some high-profile people have supported *The Red Tent*. Mickey Perlman, who publishes *What to Read: the Essential Guide for Reading Group Members and Other Book Lovers*, named *The Red Tent* as one of her favorites. Perlman leads book groups in New York and has an online book club. "'I talked a lot about it, and very enthusiastically,'" she said to Bella English. Julia Roberts chose it as a book that changed her life in Oprah Winfrey's *O* magazine, and Anita Diamant was featured in the September 2002 issue of *O* talking about her early reading experiences.

By February 2000 the novel was on its eighth printing, making a total of 185,000 paperback copies. It entered the *New York Times* bestseller lists for fiction paperbacks in December 2000, coming in at number 16 and remaining on the list for more than one year. It was still at 15 in March 2002. In September 2001 the Picador edition was the number one amazon.com paperback (*Seattle Times*, September 16, 2001). *Publishers Weekly*'s annual round-up of book sales records the paperback in its 2000 list, with sales of 471,119, and in bestsellers of 2002, with sales in that year of 438,379. Over a period of three or four years, *The Red Tent* sold steadily, rarely disappearing from book charts.

Success has not been confined to the United States. It has editions, many in translation, available in at least 20 countries, including Australia, Finland, France, Germany, Israel, Korea, Spain, and Portugal. Film rights have been sold to Palomar Pictures, a film company in California (anitadiamant.com). It was published in Great Britain in November 2001 in hardcover by Macmillan and as a Pan paperback in March 2002. Alex Clark interviewed Diamant for the Saturday Review section of the *Guardian* when the paperback came out. *The Red Tent* was by then on its twenty-second reprint and had sold in all 1.7 million copies.

British reviewers were on the whole receptive, but the novel was often seen as a book for female readers, maybe even female readers of a feminist persuasion. In the *Observer*, Nina Caplan found it an "unsubtle but intensely moving rewrite"; Diamant created a "riveting tale," but she noted the "feminist slant." The *Mail on Sunday*'s Anthony Gardner, in one of few British reviews of the hardcover, focused more explicitly on feminism, calling it "literally a feminist Bible" and situating it alongside Rebecca Wells' *Divine Secrets of the Ya-Ya Sisterhood*. He also remarks, as had some other commentators, on Diamant's representation of the biblical male characters: "Few . . . emerge well." The perception is that *The Red Tent* is a women's book that is not for "outsiders" (that is, male readers). That could be reinforced by the very positive brief review in the women's magazine, *She*, which credited it with "mesmerizing storytelling" and concluded that the novel was "[s]exy, moving and unputdownable." British sales were good, with the paperback appearing in the *Observer* bestseller charts at the end of March 2002 at number five.

If many literary reviewers were reluctant to comment on *The Red Tent*, readers have made up for them. The novel has meant a great deal to its readers, who have expressed their views in numerous ways. Diamant has been made well aware of the devotion of her readers, as she told Alex Clark in the *Guardian* interview: "I've been love-bombed a lot by my readers . . . I feel very well taken care of by them." As Lauren R. Taylor pointed out in an article for the *Washington Post*, the novel, in celebrating women's relationships, "taps into the yearning some women have for such connections, inspires them to create more, and affirms the ones that exist." Taylor identifies a craving among isolated contemporary women for the kind of nurturing community offered to Dinah by the women around her. She affirms the life-changing possibilities of the novel through the story of one reader, a "stay-at-home mother of three," who created a "birth circle," called the Red Tent, in which a group of women, some professionally qualified, give support to mothers. The many book groups in which women come across the novel also serve for some as a modern version of a red tent, a sanctuary of relaxation in female company.

Christian and Jewish readers may have been the first to show interest in the novel but even those ignorant of the Bible find inspiration and consolation in it. Diamant assumes that no biblical knowledge is required: "The whole point is that you should be able to read the book without knowing a thing" (Clark). The many reviews and comments from readers on websites show that women of all kinds have been reading the novel. Even so, detractors are to be found. Some are disturbed by the suspicion of sacrilege in the biblical rewritings; others, male and female, find the concentration on the processes of female body too much to take. The eulogies, however, are dominant from readers who have responded in an intensely personal way to the characters and their stories. Paula Day, in *Copperfield Review*, which is an online journal of historical fiction, began her review: "I have been an avid reader all of my life, but it has been years since I have had such a strong connection to a novel." Readers whose comments are cited on newvision-psychic.com talk of the comfort and guidance they have taken from the novel and of their desire to spread the word to others. On the booksellers' sites amazon.com and amazon.co.uk similar ideas are expressed. A customer from Oxfordshire, who calls herself "rutta," said: "How wonderful to remember such a time when women were so in tune with each other that they bled together every full moon. . . . This book is a delight, a fine curl-up on the sofa novel with a high feel-good factor and a blatant dose of girl-power. . . . Read this, then pass it on to your girlfriends, they will thank you for it" (amazon.co.uk, review posted March 23, 2003). Both nostalgia for a time believed to be lost where women could connect with one another and a sense of the contemporary relevance of Dinah are evoked by *The Red Tent*. A strong emotional response is obvious in many. For example, "ashananra" from Switzerland wrote: "This is only the second book that has moved me to tears at the end" (amazon.co.uk, review posted September 10, 2002). Women have loved the book so much that they have set up "Red Tent" groups simply to discuss it.

The success of *The Red Tent* may also be gauged by its imitators. Angela Elwell Hunt's *The Shadow Women* (2002) mentions *The Red Tent* on the book jacket. India Edghill's *Queenmaker* (1999) was reviewed in *Kirkus Reviews* as "in the tradition of Anita Diamant's *The Red Tent*"; Edghill has the same publisher and the same editor as Diamant had for her first novel.

Further Reading and Discussion Questions

Study Guides

Rabbi Laurie Katz Braun, "Significant Jewish Books: *The Red Tent*," http://uahc.org/books/diamant.shtml

Reading Group Guide, Picador, http://picadorusa.com/picador/rgg/redtentrgg.html

Other Novels by Women Writers referred to in Earlier Chapters

Sally Beauman, *Rebecca's Tale* (London: Little, Brown, 2001)—based on Daphne du Maurier's *Rebecca*.

Jenny Diski, *Only Human* (London: Virago, 2000)—the story of Sarai and Abram from Genesis.

Daphne du Maurier, *Rebecca* (London: Victor Gollanz, 1938).

India Edghill, *Queenmaker* (New York: Picador, 1999)—the story of Michal, King David's queen, from the Old Testament, 1 Samuel.

Susan Hill, *Mrs. de Winter* (London: Sinclair-Stevenson, 1993)—a sequel to *Rebecca*.

Angela Elwell Hunt, *The Shadow Women* (New York: Warner, 2002)—based on the story of Moses from the Old Testament, Exodus.

Jean Rhys, *Wide Sargasso Sea* (London: André Deutsch, 1966)—from Charlotte Bronte's *Jane Eyre*.

The Biblical Source for The Red Tent

The story from the arrival of Jacob up to the rape of Dinah and its consequences is in Genesis 29–35. Joseph's story is in Genesis 37 and 39–50. The following passages are from the King James version of the Bible.

GENESIS 30 (EXTRACT)—THE BIRTH OF DINAH

1: And when Rachel saw that she bare Jacob no children, Rachel envied her sister; and said unto Jacob, Give me children, or else I die.

2: And Jacob's anger was kindled against Rachel: and he said, Am I in God's stead, who hath withheld from thee the fruit of the womb?

3: And she said, Behold my maid Bilhah, go in unto her; and she shall bear upon my knees that I may also have children by her.

4: And she gave him Bilhah her handmaid to wife: and Jacob went in unto her.

5: And Bilhah conceived, and bare Jacob a son.

6: And Rachel said, God hath judged me, and hath also heard my voice, and hath given me a son: therefore called she his name Dan.

7: And Bilhah Rachel's maid conceived again, and bare Jacob a second son.

8: And Rachel said, With great wrestlings have I wrestled with my sister, and I have prevailed: and she called his name Naphtali.

9: When Leah saw that she had left bearing, she took Zilpah her maid, and gave her Jacob to wife.

10: And Zilpah Leah's maid bare Jacob a son.

11: And Leah said, A troop cometh: and she called his name Gad.

12: And Zilpah Leah's maid bare Jacob a second son.

13: And Leah said, Happy am I, for the daughters will call me blessed: and she called his name Asher.

14: And Reuben went in the days of wheat harvest, and found mandrakes in the field, and brought them unto his mother Leah. Then Rachel said to Leah, Give me, I pray thee, of thy son's mandrakes.

15: And she said unto her, Is it a small matter that thou hast taken my husband? and wouldest thou take away my son's mandrakes also? And Rachel said, Therefore he shall lie with thee to night for thy son's mandrakes.

16: And Jacob came out of the field in the evening, and Leah went out to meet him, and said, Thou must come in unto me; for surely I have hired thee with my son's mandrakes. And he lay with her that night.

17: And God hearkened unto Leah, and she conceived, and bare Jacob the fifth son.

18: And Leah said, God hath given me my hire, because I have given my maiden to my husband: and she called his name Issachar.

19: And Leah conceived again, and bare Jacob the sixth son.

20: And Leah said, God hath endued me with a good dowry; now will my husband dwell with me, because I have born him six sons: and she called his name Zebulun.

21: And afterwards she bare a daughter, and called her name Dinah.

22: And God remembered Rachel, and God hearkened to her, and opened her womb.

23: And she conceived, and bare a son; and said, God hath taken away my reproach:

24: And she called his name Joseph; and said, The LORD shall add to me another son.

GENESIS 34—THE RAPE OF DINAH (King James version)

1: And Dinah the daughter of Leah, which she bare unto Jacob, went out to see the daughters of the land.

2: And when Shechem the son of Hamor the Hivite, prince of the country, saw her, he took her, and lay with her, and defiled her.

3: And his soul clave unto Dinah the daughter of Jacob, and he loved the damsel, and spake kindly unto the damsel.

4: And Shechem spake unto his father Hamor, saying, Get me this damsel to wife.

5: And Jacob heard that he had defiled Dinah his daughter: now his sons were with his cattle in the field: and Jacob held his peace until they were come.

6: And Hamor the father of Shechem went out unto Jacob to commune with him.

7: And the sons of Jacob came out of the field when they heard it: and the men were grieved, and they were very wroth, because he had wrought folly in Israel in lying with Jacob's daughter; which thing ought not to be done.

8: And Hamor communed with them, saying, The soul of my son Shechem longeth for your daughter: I pray you give her him to wife.

9: And make ye marriages with us, and give your daughters unto us, and take our daughters unto you.

10: And ye shall dwell with us: and the land shall be before you; dwell and trade ye therein, and get you possessions therein.

11: And Shechem said unto her father and unto her brethren, Let me find grace in your eyes, and what ye shall say unto me I will give.

12: Ask me never so much dowry and gift, and I will give according as ye shall say unto me: but give me the damsel to wife.

13: And the sons of Jacob answered Shechem and Hamor his father deceitfully, and said, because he had defiled Dinah their sister:

14: And they said unto them, We cannot do this thing, to give our sister to one that is uncircumcised; for that were a reproach unto us:

15: But in this will we consent unto you: If ye will be as we be, that every male of you be circumcised;

16: Then will we give our daughters unto you, and we will take your daughters to us, and we will dwell with you, and we will become one people.

17: But if ye will not hearken unto us, to be circumcized; then will we take our daughter, and we will be gone.

18: And their words pleased Hamor, and Shechem Hamor's son.

19: And the young man deferred not to do the thing, because he had delight in Jacob's daughter: and he was more honorable than all the house of his father.

20: And Hamor and Shechem his son came unto the gate of their city, and communed with the men of their city, saying,

21: These men are peaceable with us; therefore let them dwell in the land, and trade therein; for the land, behold, it is large enough for them; let us take their daughters to us for wives, and let us give them our daughters.

22: Only herein will the men consent unto us for to dwell with us, to be one people, if every male among us be circumcized, as they are circumcized.

23: Shall not their cattle and their substance and every beast of theirs be ours? Only let us consent unto them, and they will dwell with us.

24: And unto Hamor and unto Shechem his son hearkened all that went out of the gate of his city; and every male was circumcized, all that went out of the gate of his city.

25: And it came to pass on the third day, when they were sore, that two of the sons of Jacob, Simeon and Levi, Dinah's brethren, took each man his sword, and came upon the city boldly, and slew all the males.

26: And they slew Hamor and Shechem his son with the edge of the sword, and took Dinah out of Shechem's house, and went out.

27: The sons of Jacob came upon the slain, and spoiled the city, because they had defiled their sister.

28: They took their sheep, and their oxen, and their asses, and that which was in the city, and that which was in the field,

29: And all their wealth, and all their little ones, and their wives took they captive, and spoiled even all that was in the house.

30: And Jacob said to Simeon and Levi, Ye have troubled me to make me to stink among the inhabitants of the land, among the Canaanites and the Perizzites: and I being few in number, they shall gather themselves together against me, and slay me; and I shall be destroyed, I and my house.

31: And they said, Should he deal with our sister as with an harlot?

Discussion Questions

1. *The Red Tent* has attracted a largely female readership. Although Diamant has said that she does not write specifically for women, the novel is one from which some male readers have felt excluded. Is it desirable or not to write fiction that appeals more to one sex than the other? Is it in fact inevitable that writing is gendered to the extent that writers tend to focus on personal experience to give authenticity to their writing? Are there any examples of novels of male experience that seem to exclude women in a similar way? You might consider such novels as Herman Melville's *Moby Dick* or Ernest Hemingway's *The Old Man and the Sea*. How are such novels generally viewed?

2. The most important theme in the novel is probably the value of friendship between women. How is that friendship represented? Does it have limits? What are the benefits for characters that have close female friends? What happens to those women who do not have the support of a female network?

3. How far would you agree with the criticism made by some reviewers of the novel that the male characters in *The Red Tent* are limited and stereotypical? Discuss Dinah's brothers. Are they all the same or can they be distinguished as individuals? What is your view of Shalem and Benia? Do you think that they are "token" decent men in a world of brutes, or does Diamant present a realistic range of male personalities and behavior?

4. Consider intimate relationships between men and women in the novel. How do they compare with relationships between the women? Do they seem less important or just different? Who do you think matters more to Dinah, Benia or Meryt?

5. Discuss Dinah's relationship with each of her four mothers. What does she gain or learn from them? What are the differences in their treatment of her? How important do you think her early life with Leah, Rachel, Zilpah, and Bilhah is to her development?

6. How would you describe the approach to mothering taken by the women in the novel? Compare it with contemporary experiences of motherhood. Do you think Diamant is suggesting an ideal of motherhood in Part One of the novel?

7. Do you think it is necessary to have read Genesis in order to appreciate fully *The Red Tent*? What can be learned by comparing Diamant's novel with the biblical stories? Is the Bible in any way a distraction from the novel? Does reading *The Red Tent* provoke an interest in reading, or rereading, the Bible?

8. Try reading the two novels referred to in Chapter 1 that also take marginalized women from biblical stories as their inspiration: India Edghill's *Queenmaker* and Angela Elwell Hunt's *Shadow Women*. Are these novels more or less successful than *The Red Tent*? Examine the reasons for your preferences. What makes a novel a good read?

9. Reviewers have been divided in their assessment of Diamant's writing style, with some finding its simplicity graceful and elegant, and others lamenting its straightforwardness and lack of subtlety. How do you rate Diamant's skill as a writer of prose? What contribution to the overall effect of the novel does style make? Would *The Red Tent* be as successful if it were written, for example, in the style of Henry James?

10. As was pointed out in Chapter 2, most of the characters in the novel do not worship the God of the Bible, but instead have allegiance to the host of ancient gods and goddesses known at the time. How important do you think belief in gods, and an appreciation of spirituality, is to the characters, especially the female ones? What functions do the major goddesses have in their everyday lives? For a Jewish or a Christian reader, could the representation of El, the God of the Bible, as one among many gods, be potentially offensive? Why do you think that Diamant, herself a committed Jew, chose to write about religious belief in this way?

11. What is your view of Rebecca? Dinah never loves her and others treat her with respect rather than affection. Do you think she is a genuine healer and prophet, or merely an angry, bitter woman?

12. At the end of Part Two (pp. 248–250) Dinah tells briefly of the deaths of Leah, Zilpah, and Rachel, and of the disappearance of Bilhah. All of the mothers end their lives in horrifying ways. Rachel is hastily buried after a painful death. Leah loses her dignity through paralysis. Zilpah is driven to her death when Jacob smashes the household gods. Bilhah is struck by Jacob and later leaves unnoticed. Is this account shocking or

disappointing for the reader? Given Dinah's love for her mothers, how might you explain the fact that she makes few references to them in Part Three? What does the conclusion of Part Two tell us about the changes in the lives of Jacob's women after Dinah leaves? Has Dinah's curse on Jacob and her brothers affected even her mothers or are other factors responsible for the breakdown of the women's community?

13. How effectively does Diamant establish the cultural differences between life at Haran, Shechem, and Egypt? What kinds of information does she give about the daily life of the people, and what do these details tell the reader?

14. Despite the tragedies she has suffered, Dinah maintains a buoyant outlook at the end of her life. What has she learned that enables her to survive and be happy into old age?

15. The ending of the novel is unusual in that it breaks the bounds of realism to allow Dinah to continue telling her story after her death. Discuss the significance of Dinah's apparent immortality.

Bibliography

Books by Anita Diamant

The New Jewish Wedding (New York: Simon and Schuster, 1985; revised edition 2001).

The New Jewish Baby Book (1988; reissued Woodstock, Vermont: Jewish Lights, 1994).

with Howard Cooper. *Living a Jewish Life: Jewish Traditions, Customs and Values for Today's Families* (New York: HarperCollins, 1993).

Bible Baby Names (Woodstock, Vermont: Jewish Lights, 1996).

Choosing a Jewish Life: A Handbook for People Converting to Judaism and for their Family and Friends (New York: Schocken, 1997).

The Red Tent (New York: St Martins Press, 1997).

Saying Kaddish: How to Comfort the Dying, Bury the Dead and Mourn as a Jew (New York: Schocken, 1998).

with Karen Kushner. *How to be a Jewish Parent* (New York: Schocken, 2000).

Good Harbor (New York: Simon and Schuster, 2001).

Pitching My Tent: On Marriage, Motherhood, Friendship and Other Leaps of Faith (New York: Scribner, 2003).

Interviews/Profiles

Alex Clark, "A Life in Writing: Rewriting the Good Book," *Guardian*, March 30, 2002, p. 11.

Anita Diamant and James Carroll, "Eavesdropping," *Book*, http://www.bookmagazine.com/issue19/eavesdropping.shtml.

Anita Diamant, "Author Chat," January 2, 2002, *Washington Post online*, http://discuss.washingtonpost.com/wp-srv/zforum/01/author_diamant010101.htm.

Bella English, "Pitching her 'Tent': Word of Mouth Plus Author Anita Diamant's Promotional Moxie, Make for Success," *Boston Globe*, February 24, 2000, Living Section, p. F1.

Ronnie Friedland, "Interview with Anita Diamant," *InterfaithFamily.com*, http://www.interfaithfamily.com/article/issue73/friedland.phtml.

Jodi Gilman, "Anita Diamant: Writing into the Silence," *Tufts Observer online*, http://ase.tufts.edu/observer/news4.html.

Jessica Jernigan, "Timeless Women and Timely Concerns," *Borders.com*, http://www.bordersstores.com/ib/200111/ib_features_diamant.jsp.

Faith L Justice, "An Interview with Anita Diamant," *Copperfield Review*, http://www.copperfieldreview.com/interviews/diamant.html.

Ellen Kanner, "Very Interesting People: Anita Diamant," *BookSense.com*, http://www.booksense.com/people/archive/diamantanita.jsp.

Suzanne Mantell, "The Importance of Friends," *Publisher's Weekly*, May 3, 2002.

Rahel Musleah, "Profile of Anita Diamant," *InterfaithFamily.com*, http://www.interfaithfamily.com/article/issue61/musleah.phtml.

Irene Sege, "A Handbook for 'Jews by Choice': Anita Diamant Pens a Guide for Converts," *Boston Globe*, June 5, 1997, Living section, p. E1.

Lauren R. Taylor, "'Red Tent': Well-Received Wisdom for Women," *Washington Post*, March 1, 2001, p. C4.

Reviews of The Red Tent

Anon, "Anita Diamant's *The Red Tent*," *City Beat*, 7, 26 (May 17–23), 2001.
Anon, "Review," *She*, September 2001.

Nina Caplan, "Paperbacks Review," *Observer*, March 3, 2002, p.18.

Paula Day, *"The Red Tent," Copperfield Review*, http://www.copperfield review.com/reviews/red_tent.html.

Bonnie V. Fetterman, "Significant Jewish Books," *Reform Judaism Magazine*, 27, 4, Summer 1999, p. 48.

Anthony Gardner, "The Women-Only Gospel," *Mail on Sunday*, November 11, 2001, p. 66.

Merle Rubin, "Memory and Imagination Reclaim the Past," *Christian Science Monitor*, 27 January 1998.

Reviews of Good Harbor

Anon, "In Brief: Guilt and Grace," *Washington Post*, November 18, 2001, p. T12.

Sandy Bauers, "Diamant's Done Better but *Good Harbor* Suits," *Philadelphia Inquirer*, January 13, 2002, p. H14.

Karen Campbell, "Diamant's Latest: Two Chicks Dishing," *Boston Globe*, December 16, 2001, p. D5.

Kim Germovsek, "Seaworthy, Despite a Few Leaks," *Post-Gazette.com*, October 21, 2001.

Jemima Hunt, "Review: Paperback Fiction," *Guardian*, October 19, 2002, p. 30.

Sally Morris, "Reviews: Books," *Sunday Mirror*, October 13, 2002, Features, p. 52.

Merle Rubin, "Women who Shelter Each Other," *Christian Science Monitor*, October 11, 2001.

Valerie Ryan, *"Good Harbor* is Page Turner," *Seattle Times*, December 16, 2001.

Robin Vidimos, "Exploring Bonds of Friendship: Emotional Insight elevates *Good Harbor*," *Denver Post*, October 7, 2001, Books section, p. FF-02.

Geoffrey Wansell, "New Fiction," *Daily Mail*, October 18, 2002, p. 58.

Judith Wynn, "Women's Friendship Frames *Good Harbor*," *Boston Herald*, November 25, 2001.

Websites

http://www.anitadiamant.com (author's official website).
http:/www.newvision-psychic.com/bookshelf/RedTent.htm (readers' reviews).

Critical Material

Judy Grahn, *Blood, Bread and Roses: How Menstruation Created the World* (Boston: Beacon Press, 1993).

Maggie Humm, *The Dictionary of Feminist Theory* (Hemel Hempstead: Harvester Wheatsheaf, 1989).

Jordan Paper, *Through the Earth Darkly: Female Spirituality in Comparative Perspective* (New York: Continuum, 1997).

Adrienne Rich, *Of Woman Born: Motherhood as Experience and Institution* (London: Virago, 1977).

Elaine Showalter, *A Literature of Their Own* (Princeton, NJ: Princeton University Press, 1977).

Elaine Showalter, *The Female Malady: Women, Madness and English Culture, 1830–1980* (London: Virago, 1987).